D0036993

TO:

Ronald LeRoy Mauck IV

FROM:

Lisa Ann Villarreal & Ronald LeRoy Mauck, Jr

DATE:

Eternal

UNSHAKABLE HOPE

PROMISE BOOK

STUDENT EDITION

MAX LUCADO

WITH ALLEN ARNOLD

THOMAS NELSON
Since 1798

© 2018 Max Lucado

All rights reserved. No portion of this book may be reproduced, stored in a retrieval system, or transmitted in any form or by any means—electronic, mechanical, photocopy, recording, scanning, or other—except for brief quotations in critical reviews or articles, without the prior written permission of the publisher.

Published in Nashville, Tennessee, by Thomas Nelson. Thomas Nelson is a registered trademark of HarperCollins Christian Publishing, Inc.

Thomas Nelson titles may be purchased in bulk for educational, business, fundraising, or sales promotional use. For information, please e-mail SpecialMarkets@ThomasNelson.com.

Unless otherwise noted, Scripture quotations are taken from the Holy Bible, New International Version®, NIV®. Copyright © 1973, 1978, 1984, 2011 by Biblica, Inc.® Used by permission of Zondervan. All rights reserved worldwide. www.zondervan.com. The "NIV" and "New International Version" are trademarks registered in the United States Patent and Trademark Office by Biblica, Inc.®

Other Scripture references are from the following sources: New American Standard Bible® (NASB), Copyright © 1960, 1962, 1963, 1968, 1971, 1972, 1973, 1975, 1977, 1995 by The Lockman Foundation. Used by permission. (www.Lockman.org) *The Message* (THE MESSAGE). Copyright © by Eugene H. Peterson 1993, 1994, 1995, 1996, 2000, 2001, 2002. Used by permission of NavPress. All rights reserved. Represented by Tyndale House Publishers, Inc. New Century Version® (NCV). © 2005 by Thomas Nelson. Used by permission. All rights reserved. New King James Version® (NKJV). © 1982 by Thomas Nelson. Used by permission. All rights reserved. *Holy Bible*, New Living Translation (NLT). © 1996, 2004, 2007, 2013 by Tyndale House Foundation. Used by permission of Tyndale House Publishers, Inc., Carol Stream, Illinois 60188. All rights reserved. The Living Bible (TLB). Copyright © 1971. Used by permission of Tyndale House Publishers, Inc., Carol Stream, Illinois 60188. All rights reserved.

ISBN: 978-1-4003-1661-8

Library of Congress Cataloging-in-Publication Data is on file.

Printed in the United States of America

18 19 20 21 22 LSC 6 5 4 3 2 1

Denalyn and I proudly dedicate this
volume to Maxine Nadeau—celebrating
her tireless devotion to students

CONTENTS

NOTE FROM THE AUTHOR

What's shaking your world right now? Your future? Your faith? Maybe it's your family or your friendships. Does it sometimes feel as if it's everything all at once?

If you could use some unshakable hope, I've got good news: God's promises are bigger than any problem you'll ever face.

After a few decades of following Jesus, I've discovered that nothing gives me more hope than God's promises. Our mighty and loving God governs the world according to his promises. In this book I've included thirty of my favorite go-to promises. Throughout the years I've turned to these promises to encourage others—and to encourage myself. You and I desperately need them.

Just as the doctor might prescribe a medication for your body, God has given promises for your heart. These are meant to help you cope with your problems, fears, and questions. They will set your mind at ease and remind you that God has everything under control.

God's promises will also remind you that you aren't alone. I know it can feel like you are at times. But God is with you, and he loves you more than you can imagine.

In a shaky world, that's the best promise of all: you can find unshakable hope in the God who promises always to love you and never leave you.

MAX LUCADO

GOD KEEPS HIS PROMISES

[God] has given us his very great and precious promises, so that through them you may participate in the divine nature.

—2 PETER 1:4

If you believe in the promises of God, you're in good company. The heroes in the Bible were all ages and came from all cultures. Some of them were rich and others were poor. Yet they had one thing in common: they built their lives on the promises of God.

Because of God's promises, Noah believed in rain before a single drop had ever fallen on earth. Because of God's promises, Abraham left a good home for one he'd never seen. Because of God's promises, Joshua led two million people into the promised land. Because of God's promises, David conked a giant, Peter rebounded from regret, and Paul found a grace worth dying for.

God's promises were guiding truths in their journeys of faith—and they had plenty of promises to pick from. One student of the Bible spent a year and a half attempting to count the number of promises God made to humanity. He came up with 7,487 promises![1]

Not only is God a promise maker; God is a promise keeper. From Genesis 1, the Bible makes the case that we can depend on God. Nine times the text repeats "God said." And without exception, when God spoke, something wonderful happened. By divine order, he made light, land, beaches, and creatures. God didn't discuss it with any advisors. He needed no help. He spoke, and it happened. We're left with one conclusion: God's word is guaranteed. What he says happens.

FAITH IS THE DEEPLY HELD BELIEF THAT GOD WILL KEEP HIS PROMISES.

Faith is the deeply held belief that God will keep his promises. God will not—he cannot—break his promises. What he says will happen.

It must happen! God's promises are irrevocable because of who he is:

- **God is unchanging.** He sees the end from the beginning. He's never caught off guard or surprised. He makes no course corrections. He is not swayed by up-and-down moods. "He never changes" (James 1:17 NLT).
- **God is faithful.** "God can be trusted to keep his promise" (Hebrews 10:23 NLT).
- **God is strong.** He does not overpromise and underdeliver. "God is able to do whatever he promises" (Romans 4:21 NLT).
- **God cannot lie.** "It is impossible for God to lie" (Hebrews 6:18 NLT). A rock cannot swim. A hippo cannot fly. A butterfly cannot eat a bowl of spaghetti. You cannot sleep on a cloud, and God cannot lie. He never exaggerates, manipulates, fibs, or flatters. "He doesn't break promises!" (Titus 1:2 THE MESSAGE).

The question is not whether God keeps his promises. The question is, will you build your life upon them?

GOD'S PROMISES FOR YOU

The LORD said: "I am making a covenant with you. Before all your people I will do wonders never before done in any nation in all the world. The people you live among will see how awesome is the work that I, the LORD, will do for you."

EXODUS 34:10

"As the rain and snow come down from heaven and stay upon the ground to water the earth, and cause the grain to grow and to produce seed for the farmer and bread for the hungry, so also is my word. I send it out, and it always produces fruit. It shall accomplish all I want it to and prosper everywhere I send it."

ISAIAH 55:10-11 TLB

The promise is targeted to you and your children, but also to all who are far away—whomever, in fact, our Master God invites.

ACTS 2:39 THE MESSAGE

God is able to do whatever he promises.

ROMANS 4:21 NLT

No matter how many promises God has made, they are "Yes" in Christ. And so through him the "Amen" is spoken by us to the glory of God.

2 CORINTHIANS 1:20

Let's keep a firm grip on the promises that keep us going. He always keeps his word.

HEBREWS 10:23 THE MESSAGE

The Lord is not slow in doing what he promised—the way some people understand slowness. But God is being patient with you. He does not want anyone to be lost, but he wants all people to change their hearts and lives.

2 PETER 3:9 NCV

THINK AND RESPOND

This chapter defined faith as "the deeply held belief that God will keep his promises." Right now in your life is it easy to believe that God will keep his promises? Or is it difficult? Why?

Which characteristics of God, some of which were mentioned in this chapter, do you need to be reminded of in your current circumstances?

Describe a time in your life when nothing seemed to be going right but God gave you hope.

Write a Bible verse from this chapter that will help you remember that God is a promise maker and a promise keeper.

MY PROMISE TO GOD

I will build my life on God's promises. In a shaky world, I will trust God's unshakable Word. Rather than focusing on my circumstances and problems, I will place my hope in God and his promises.

YOU CAN KNOW GOD

"All people will know me."

—HEBREWS 8:11 NCV

God guarantees a day when all people who want to know him will do so. Even now, God is revealing himself, inviting us to take a glimpse. We can know more than simple facts about him; we can know his heart, his joy, his passion, his plan, and his sorrows. God wants us to know *him*.

Some years ago my wife and I had a wilderness adventure in the Rocky Mountains . . . well, it was really more like a five-mile hike on a well-paved trail. Carrying a backpack filled with peanut butter sandwiches and two jugs of water, we trekked through pine trees and mountain rocks. By the time we got to the breathtaking waterfalls, we were out of breath. A sign invited hikers to keep going, but we were worn out. We didn't camp out. We didn't see wild animals. We didn't even build a campfire. Instead, we walked back to civilization to get sandwiches from the local deli. Such was the extent of my mountain-climbing experience!

As soon as I got off the trail, I did what you might expect: I ordered business cards with my new title—Max Lucado, Mountain Man. I got an office, hung a Wilderness Expert sign on the door, and offered my wisdom to anyone who needed it.

Would you hire me as an adventure guide? Of course not! You'd laugh at me, report me, or maybe try to correct me, but you wouldn't ask me for advice. After all, I didn't even make it all the way up the mountain!

When it comes to knowledge of God, we can't claim to be experts. Our finest thoughts are first grade math to his advanced algebra. We will never know everything about him. God is beyond our biggest thoughts, but that shouldn't discourage us. Once we are in heaven, we will enjoy an eternal adventure of discovery. We'll never stop learning about God and how amazing he is.

But we don't have to wait that long; we can begin now. In fact, the mark of a person who loves God is that he or she is always growing in the knowledge of God. "Don't let the rich brag of their riches. If you brag, brag of this and this only: That you understand and know me" (Jeremiah 9:23–24 THE MESSAGE).

WE CAN KNOW GOD. HE HAS NOT HIDDEN HIMSELF FROM US.

The facts lead to a wonderful conclusion: we can know God. He has not hidden himself from us. He doesn't close the door on his children. He doesn't refuse our questions. He promises to make himself known to all who search for him.

GOD'S PROMISES FOR YOU

The heavens declare the glory of God,
and the skies announce what his hands have made.
Day after day they tell the story;
night after night they tell it again.
They have no speech or words;
they have no voice to be heard.
But their message goes out through all the world;
their words go everywhere on earth.

PSALM 19:1–4 NCV

Wise men and women are always learning,
always listening for fresh insights.

PROVERBS 18:15 THE MESSAGE

"I'll show you how great I am, how holy I am. I'll make myself known all over the world. Then you'll realize that I am GOD."

EZEKIEL 38:23 THE MESSAGE

What may be known about God is plain to them, because God has made it plain to them. For since the creation of the world God's invisible qualities—His eternal power and divine nature—have been clearly seen, being understood from what has been made, so that people are without excuse.

ROMANS 1:19-20

Oh, the depth of the riches of the wisdom and knowledge
of God!
How unsearchable his judgments, and his paths beyond
tracing out!
"Who has known the mind of the Lord?
Or who has been his counselor?"
"Who has ever given to God,
that God should repay them?"
For from him and through him and for him are all things.
To him be the glory forever! Amen.

ROMANS 11:33-36

THINK AND RESPOND

How does knowing more about God help you understand more about your life?

Do you feel you know mostly facts about God or that you know him personally? What are some ways you can get to know God more this week?

What questions do you look forward to asking God one day?

List several things you've learned about God that you think are amazing, and share why these things mean so much to you.

MY PROMISE TO GOD

I will make knowing God my main goal. Rather than just study facts about God, I will spend time with God himself. Through reading the Bible and spending time with him in prayer, I will begin the adventure of knowing God personally.

YOU ARE GOD'S IDEA

Let us make human beings in our image,
make them reflecting our nature.

—GENESIS 1:26 THE MESSAGE

Every person has asked themselves the same question: *Am I somebody important?*

It's easy to feel unimportant when the school sees you as a number, your friend is rude to you, and your parents don't understand you. But when you struggle with that question, remember this promise of God: you were created by God, in God's image, for God's glory. You are important to him.

> God spoke: "Let us make human beings in our image, make them reflecting our nature so they can be responsible for the fish in the sea, the birds in the air, the cattle, and, yes, Earth itself, and every animal that moves on the face of Earth." (Genesis 1:26 THE MESSAGE)

Within these words is the most wonderful of promises: God made us to reflect the image of God.

To be clear: no one is a god. Only God is God. But everyone reflects certain aspects of God. Wisdom. Love. Grace. Kindness. A longing for eternity. These are just some of the things that set us apart from animals and suggest that we resemble our Creator. We are made in *his image* and in *his likeness.*

YOU WERE CREATED BY GOD, IN GOD'S IMAGE, FOR GOD'S GLORY.

We "take after" God in many ways. There is no exception to this promise. Every person is made in the image of God.

Maybe someone called you a loser. Said you don't matter. That you're a waste of space. Don't listen to them. They don't know what they are talking about! A divine spark shines within you. When you say yes to God, you become more like him. Are you perfect? No. But you are being made perfect. He has a never-ending love for you, yet his love for you doesn't depend on you.

You are God's idea. God's child. Created in God's image.

Would you let this truth find its way into your heart? God knew you before your parents named you. You were loved in heaven before you were born on earth. You aren't an accident. You aren't defined by the number of pounds you weigh, the amount of social media followers you have, or the price of the shoes you wear.

When we were toddlers, we had a tendency to say, "Look at me!" Wanting attention is acceptable for little kids. But even as we get older, we want the same. "Look at me ace the test. Look at me wear the most expensive clothes, use big words, or flex my muscles. Look at me!"

Isn't it time we grew up? We were made to live a life that says, "Look at God!" People should look at us and see not us but the image of our Maker.

This is God's plan. This is God's promise. We do matter. We are important because God made us and is continuing to make us more and more into his image.

GOD'S PROMISES FOR YOU

This is the written account of the descendants of Adam. When God created human beings, he made them to be like himself.

GENESIS 5:1 NLT

You created my inmost being;
you knit me together in my mother's womb.
I praise you because I am fearfully and wonderfully made;
your works are wonderful,
I know that full well.

PSALM 139:13–14

[We] are being transformed into his image with ever-increasing glory, which comes from the Lord, who is the Spirit.

2 CORINTHIANS 3:18

Take on an entirely new way of life—a God-fashioned life, a life renewed from the inside and working itself into your conduct as God accurately reproduces his character in you.

EPHESIANS 4:24 THE MESSAGE

You have taken off your old self with its practices and have put on the new self, which is being renewed in knowledge in the image of its Creator.

COLOSSIANS 3:9–10

Friends, that's exactly who we are: children of God. And that's only the beginning. Who knows how we'll end up! What we know is that when Christ is openly revealed, we'll see him—and in seeing him, become like him.

1 JOHN 3:2 THE MESSAGE

THINK AND RESPOND

Do you think Adam and Eve saw God as their Father? Do you see God more as your heavenly Father or a powerful but distant God? Why?

Read this statement again: "You were loved in heaven before you were born on earth. You aren't an accident." Does this feel true? Why or why not?

Do you base your importance on what you wear, how well you do in school, or the people you hang out with? Or is your value based in who God says you are? Explain.

In what ways do you see God working in you to make you more like him? Can you see those areas as "works in progress" rather than as reasons to feel ashamed?

MY PROMISE TO GOD

I will embrace my identity as a child of God and his image bearer. I will be confident in my identity because I am his child, his idea, and he created me in his image. I will live each day becoming more like my Father.

YOU CAN OVERCOME THE ENEMY

The God who brings peace will soon defeat Satan and give you power over him.

—ROMANS 16:20 NCV

The Bible says we have an enemy called the devil. The Greek word for "devil" is *diabolos*, which means "to split."[2] The devil is a splitter, a divider, and a wedge driver. He divided Adam and Eve from God in the garden and would like to separate you from God as well.

Does talk about the devil seem outdated or make-believe to you? If so, you aren't alone. According to research from the Barna Group, most Christians refuse to believe Satan is real.[3] This must make him happy. As long as he isn't taken seriously, the devil is free to work his evil. He wants to make your life a mess and to keep his name out of it.

But God doesn't let him do so.

In the Bible Jesus had more to say about Satan than anyone else. Jesus didn't see Satan as a made-up villain. So when Jesus taught us to pray, he said, "Deliver us from the evil one" (Matthew 6:13).

SINCE SATAN COMES TO STEAL, KILL, AND DESTROY, WHEREVER YOU SEE LOSS, DEATH, OR DESTRUCTION, TURN TO GOD IN PRAYER.

We play into the devil's hand when we pretend he does not exist. The devil is a real devil.

But, and this is huge, *the devil is a defeated devil.* Were Satan to read the Bible, he would hate what he reads. Page after page makes this clear: the devil's days are numbered.

Since Satan comes to steal, kill, and destroy, wherever you see loss, death, or destruction, turn to God in prayer. Since Satan's name means "divider," you know what's going on. Remember these Bible verses and believe God's promises regarding Satan.

- "The God who brings peace will soon defeat Satan and give you power over him." (Romans 16:20 NCV)
- "God's Spirit, who is in you, is greater than the devil, who is in the world." (1 John 4:4 NCV)
- "God is faithful; he will not let you be tempted beyond what you can bear." (1 Corinthians 10:13)
- "Resist the devil, and he will flee from you." (James 4:7)

When we pray, we are using God's truth and power against the devil. When we worship, we do what Satan himself did not do: we give God authority over us. When we read Scripture, we do what Jesus did in the wilderness: he responded to Satan by quoting God's truth. And, since Satan can't stand the truth, he left Jesus alone. Satan will not hang out where God is praised and prayers are offered.

Satan is our enemy, but he is not God's equal in any way.

Life gives you lots of reasons to worry. You will make mistakes. The devil will seem to be in control. All that is good may appear to lose. But you don't need to worry. God has already won.

GOD'S PROMISES FOR YOU

The thief comes only to steal and kill and destroy; I have come that they may have life, and have it to the full.

JOHN 10:10

Do not be overcome by evil, but overcome evil with good.

ROMANS 12:21

Put on the full armor of God so that you can fight against the devil's evil tricks. Our fight is not against people on earth but against the rulers and authorities and the powers of this world's darkness, against the spiritual powers of evil in the heavenly world. That is why you need to put on God's full armor. Then on the day of evil you will be able to stand strong. And when you have finished the whole fight, you will still be standing.

EPHESIANS 6:11–13 NCV

He has rescued us from the dominion of darkness and brought us into the kingdom of the Son he loves.

COLOSSIANS 1:13

Let God work his will in you. Yell a loud *no* to the Devil and watch him scamper.

JAMES 4:7 THE MESSAGE

Be alert and of sober mind. Your enemy the devil prowls around like a roaring lion looking for someone to devour.

1 PETER 5:8

> [The devil] is filled with fury,
> because he knows that his time is short.

REVELATION 12:12

THINK AND RESPOND

Are you surprised that most Christians don't believe in the devil? Do you sometimes forget you have an enemy trying to destroy your life?

The devil's name means "divider." How has he tried to come between you and your family or you and your friends? How has he tried to separate you and God?

How did this chapter change or challenge your view of Satan? How can you apply this knowledge to whatever temptation you are facing today?

Jesus' strategy for guarding himself against Satan's lies was to recite God's Word. What scriptures do you need right now to remind yourself of God's truth? Write them down.

MY PROMISE TO GOD

I believe the devil exists, and I will resist him. I will worship God more than focus on the enemy. When Satan tempts me, I will hold firm to God and resist the devil, knowing he must flee.

GOD TAKES CARE OF YOU

"When you're in over your head, I'll be there with you."

—ISAIAH 43:2 THE MESSAGE

Everything about the Old Testament story of Noah and the ark is monumental. Big boat. Big task. But the boat and task were monumental because the floodwaters would be.

God's word to Noah was this: Build the ark. Load the animals. A flood is coming. I imagine a comedy routine in which Noah hears and responds to God's commands:

"I want you to build an ark."

"Okay. What's an ark?"

"It's a boat. Build it three hundred cubits long, fifty cubits wide, and thirty cubits high."

"Right. What's a cubit?"

"Collect all of the animals in the world."

"Who is this, really?"

"I'm going to flood the world."

"What's a flood?"

If Noah had questions like these for God, they didn't make it into the Bible. Scripture gives just a one-line summary: "Noah did everything just as God commanded him" (Genesis 6:22).

It took Noah decades to build the boat, but he finished it. No one had ever seen an ark or a rainstorm, yet Noah obeyed. And after forty days of rain and eight months of floating, Noah and his family came to rest on dry land.

God promised Noah a safe place, a guaranteed rescue. In this story of monumental boat, task, and flood is an even more monumental promise: God takes care of his people.

I wish I knew more to tell you about Noah. Was he valedictorian of his class? Was he voted Most Likely to Succeed? If only Noah had left behind a yearbook, we might know more about his accomplishments. The Bible only tells us that Noah "walked faithfully with God" (Genesis 6:9).

But maybe this is the big point. Noah didn't get an award for his work or recognition for his skill. Noah found a God who would stoop down and help him. Indeed, "stoop" is the Hebrew meaning of the word *grace*. God stooped and entered Noah's world. Grace is the God who stoops, who reaches down to help us.

GRACE IS THE GOD WHO STOOPS, WHO REACHES DOWN TO HELP US.

The promise of God through the story of Noah is this: the Lord has seen you. He has taken note of your heart and desire to follow him, and you, like Noah, have found favor in his eyes. You may not have favor in the eyes of your coach, your crush, or the most popular person in school, but you have favor in the eyes of God.

He has sent us a rescue vessel as well. In our case, we are saved not by a boat, but by Jesus Christ. We can trust him. He, and he alone, keeps us safe from the circumstances that swirl around us. When we trust the promises of God, we enjoy the unspeakable benefit of his Son.

GOD'S PROMISES FOR YOU

Noah found favor in the eyes of the Lord. This is the account of Noah and his family. Noah was a righteous man, blameless among the people of his time, and he walked faithfully with God.

GENESIS 6:8-9

"I will establish my covenant with you, and you will enter the ark—you and your sons and your wife and your sons' wives with you."

GENESIS 6:18

God said, "This is the sign of the covenant I am making between me and you and every living creature with you, a covenant for all generations to come: I have set my rainbow in the clouds, and it will be the sign of the covenant between me and the earth."

GENESIS 9:12-13

"The Father gives me the people who are mine. Every one of them will come to me, and I will always accept them."

JOHN 6:37 NCV

All have sinned and fall short of the glory of God, and all are justified freely by his grace through the redemption that came by Christ Jesus. God presented Christ as a sacrifice of atonement, through the shedding of his blood—to be received by faith. He did this to demonstrate his righteousness, because in his forbearance he had left the sins committed beforehand unpunished—he did it to demonstrate his righteousness at the present time, so as to be just and the one who justifies those who have faith in Jesus.

ROMANS 3:23-26

He is able, once and forever, to save those who come to God through him. He lives forever to intercede with God on their behalf.

HEBREWS 7:25 NLT

THINK AND RESPOND

God commanded Noah to do something that had never been done before while preparing for an event that had never occurred before. How would you respond if God told you to do something that you had no idea how to accomplish?

God provides us a way of escape as he did for Noah through the ark. Can you think of an example of how he has rescued you?

What aspect of Noah's character do you most admire? How can you be more like him in embracing God's commands?

What situation are you facing that feels overwhelming right now? What promise from God can give you hope during this time?

MY PROMISE TO GOD

I will trust God and obey his commands. When I don't understand what the Lord is doing in my life, I will respond with greater faith. And when given the option of choosing between the world's ways and God's promises, I will choose God.

FAITH MAKES YOU RIGHT WITH GOD

People are counted as righteous, not because of their work, but because of their faith in God who forgives sinners.

—ROMANS 4:5 NLT

Imagine being given a gift card to your favorite restaurant. There's $1,000 loaded on the card, so you invite all your friends out to eat and tell them to come hungry—it's on you. So they do. But when you go to pay, you realize there's a huge problem. You miscounted the zeros, and what you thought was $1,000 was really $10.

The food has been eaten, the friends have gone home, and you only have a few coins in your pocket. How can you possibly pay the debt?

If that's hard to figure, imagine trying to pay the cost of your sins. Even figuring it out is impossible. What, for example, is the charge for cheating on a test? Posting something mean about someone on social media? Lying to your parents?

What about the times when we sin and don't even know it? Do we get a free pass if we didn't know any better?

That's the real question: how do I deal with the debt I owe to God?

Deny that I owe anything? My conscience won't let me. Point out worse sins in others? God won't fall for that. Try to pay it off? I could, but that takes us back to the problem. We don't know the cost of sin. We don't even know how much we owe. So how do we pay off our debt?

God's answer will surprise you: "People are counted as righteous, not because of their work, but because of their faith in God who forgives sinners" (Romans 4:5 NLT).

Though this promise was written in the New Testament, it first appeared in the Old Testament regarding Abram. We know him today as Abraham. This promise is noteworthy because God offered everything and he required only Abraham's faith in return. It is no wonder that Abraham came to be known as the father of the faith—at the beginning, faith was all he had.

> The promise is received by faith. It is given as a free gift. And we are all certain to receive it, whether or not we live according to the law of Moses, if we have faith like Abraham's. (Romans 4:16 NLT)

Those who trust in Christ are included in the blessing of Abraham. We are seen as a part of the family. When Abraham was told his family would outnumber the stars, God was thinking of you and me.

God's promise to Abraham was he would be saved by faith. God's promise to you and me is we will be saved by our faith. Just faith.

GOD'S PROMISE TO YOU AND ME IS WE WILL BE SAVED BY OUR FAITH. JUST FAITH.

We no longer have to be afraid of falling short! Gone is the pressure to be perfect. Gone are the nagging questions: *Have I done enough? Am I good enough? Will I achieve enough?*

What's impossible for us to pay has been paid in full by God when we put our faith in him. The payment is no longer up to us. Rest in that promise.

GOD'S PROMISES FOR YOU

Abram believed the Lord, and he credited it to him as righteousness.

GENESIS 15:6

Salvation comes no other way; no other name has been or will be given to us by which we can be saved, only this one.

ACTS 4:12 THE MESSAGE

Now to the one who works, wages are not credited as a gift but as an obligation. However, to the one who does not work but trusts God who justifies the ungodly, their faith is credited as righteousness. David says the same thing when he speaks of the blessedness of the one to whom God credits righteousness apart from works:

> "Blessed are those
> whose transgressions are forgiven,
> whose sins are covered.
> Blessed is the one
> whose sin the Lord will never count against them."

ROMANS 4:4–8

I am convinced that nothing can ever separate us from God's love. Neither death nor life, neither angels nor demons, neither our fears for today nor our worries about tomorrow—not even the powers of hell can separate us from God's love. No power in the sky above or in the earth below—indeed, nothing in all creation will ever be able to separate us from the love of God that is revealed in Christ Jesus our Lord.

ROMANS 8:38–39 NLT

I am certain that God, who began the good work within you, will continue his work until it is finally finished on the day when Christ Jesus returns.

PHILIPPIANS 1:6 NLT

Every God-begotten person conquers the world's ways. The conquering power that brings the world to its knees is our faith.

1 JOHN 5:4 THE MESSAGE

THINK AND RESPOND

Are you afraid to mess up or disappoint people? If so, in what areas of your life is this a struggle?

Write Romans 4:5 (you can look it up in the Bible or find it at the beginning of this chapter).

Why is this scripture such good news? Does this promise change how you see yourself when you are tempted to compare yourself to the status or accomplishments of other people?

Why did God call Abraham the father of our faith? How does his faith inspire you to believe God's promises?

MY PROMISE TO GOD

I will remember that God has covered my debt of sin because of my faith in Jesus. Rather than fear that my sins aren't forgiven, I will be confident in God's promise that I am saved by faith alone.

GOD CAN TURN BAD THINGS INTO GOOD

"I'll see to it that everything works out for the best."

—ISAIAH 54:17 THE MESSAGE

Joseph's story in the Bible is one of abandonment. His brothers disliked his dreams, his swagger, and that Joseph was their father's favorite, so they decided to throw him into a pit and planned to kill him. The only reason they didn't was because they had a chance to sell him to passersby in need of slaves.

Joseph was placed on an Egyptian auction block and awarded to the highest bidder. But he didn't lose hope. He worked his way to the top of the household of a man named Potiphar, who was one of the Egyptian pharaoh's high-ranking officials. But then Potiphar's wife tried to flirt with Joseph, and when he said no, she accused him of doing what she had done. Potiphar took his wife's side and tossed Joseph in jail for a crime he didn't commit.

In prison Joseph met a butler—another official in the royal court—who had an unusual dream. Joseph helped him figure out what his dream meant and in exchange asked him to remember him when he got out of jail. The butler agreed but quickly forgot, and Joseph sat in prison for two years with no word, no hope, and no solution.

Two years! Plenty of time to give up. Plenty of time to give in to despair. Plenty of time to wonder: *Is this how God treats his children? Do your best and this is what you get? A jail cell and a hard bed?*

If Joseph asked such questions, we don't know. But if you ask those questions, you aren't alone. *Does God know what I'm going through? If God knows, does he care? How could this struggle fit into his plans?*

If God is in charge, why does he let challenges come your way? Wouldn't an almighty God prevent them?

Not if they are for his higher purpose. It was through suffering that Joseph came to be God's tool of rescue for the Hebrew people. Here's the rest of the story: when Pharaoh was troubled by his dreams, the butler finally remembered Joseph and recalled his promise. The butler mentioned Joseph to the pharaoh, and in the blink of an eye, Joseph went from the prison to the palace. He interpreted the pharaoh's dream as a forecast of a coming famine. Pharaoh promoted Joseph to prime minister so he could help prevent the crisis, and in doing so, Joseph saved not just the Egyptians but his family as well. Years later Joseph would tell his brothers, "You intended to harm me, but God intended it for good to accomplish what is now being done, the saving of many lives" (Genesis 50:20).

What was meant to hurt him was used for his good. Why? Because God had not forgotten Joseph. Nor has he forgotten you. I'm sorry for the pain you've experienced in your life. But if the story of Joseph teaches us anything, it is this: we have a choice. We can focus on our hurts or our hopes. Joseph chose God's promise of hope. I encourage you to do the same.

WE HAVE A CHOICE. WE CAN FOCUS ON OUR HURTS OR OUR HOPES.

GOD'S PROMISES FOR YOU

"I will be with you as I was with Moses. I will not fail you or abandon you."

JOSHUA 1:5 NLT

Is anyone crying for help? God is listening,
ready to rescue you.

PSALM 34:17 THE MESSAGE

We can rejoice, too, when we run into problems and trials, for we know that they help us develop endurance.

ROMANS 5:3 NLT

We know that in all things God works for the good of those who love him, who have been called according to his purpose.

ROMANS 8:28

He comforts us in all our troubles so that we can comfort others. When they are troubled, we will be able to give them the same comfort God has given us.

2 CORINTHIANS 1:4 NLT

In Christ we were chosen to be God's people, because from the very beginning God had decided this in keeping with his plan. And he is the One who makes everything agree with what he decides and wants.

EPHESIANS 1:11 NCV

My friends, do not be surprised at the terrible trouble which now comes to test you. Do not think that something strange is happening to you. But be happy that you are sharing in Christ's sufferings so that you will be happy and full of joy when Christ comes again in glory.

1 PETER 4:12–13 NCV

THINK AND RESPOND

How would you answer these questions? *Does God know what I'm going through? If God knows, does he care? How could these circumstances fit into his plans for me?*

Joseph was betrayed by his brothers and unfairly imprisoned for two years. Did he seem to give up hope during that time? Why do you think that?

In the middle of difficult circumstances, it's easy to feel abandoned by others and by God. Yet in Joshua 1:5, God promised never to abandon you. Find the verse in this chapter, and write it in the space below.

Romans 8:28 promises that God actively works for the good of those who love him all—not some of—the time. What might God be doing to bring good from bad in a struggle you're facing?

MY PROMISE TO GOD

I will trust God during difficult times. Even when it feels like he has forgotten me or left me alone, I know God will see me through the hard times—every time.

GOD'S WORD WILL GUIDE YOU

I will instruct you and teach you in the way you should go; I will counsel you with my loving eye on you.

—PSALM 32:8

My to-do list for my first day in heaven reads as follows:

- Worship Jesus.
- Hug my dad, mom, my brother, and sisters.
- Thank those who prayed for me when I was far from God.

Then I'd like to have a long talk with Moses. I imagine the wooly-haired man with the same staff that once became a snake and then became a staff again. We'd sit down at the Pearly Gates sidewalk café, and I would start by asking him about the biggest moment of his earthly life.

"Hmm, so many moments to choose from. The burning bush that never burned up. The ten plagues—my favorite was the hopping frogs. Pharaoh saw them and nearly croaked." (I never knew Moses was so funny.)

At that point he will look at me and, from beneath that grizzly, salt-and-pepper beard, smile. He will stand from his chair, hold the staff with one hand, and lift a finger into the air with the other. And, as if he is writing on an invisible tablet, he will say, "The finger in the stone. That's it. The moment when God's finger carved the Ten Commandments into the stone."

We'll have to wait to hear the actual answer from Moses. But a strong case can be made for the Ten Commandments moment. I envision God's lightning-like finger chiseling word after word into stone. If Moses was able to move, it was only to gulp or pray as God wrote the words. When done, the stone tablets were given to Moses, and he gave them to the people.

In doing so, God gave us this promise: he will guide us! "I will instruct you and teach you in the way you should go" (Psalm 32:8). His words of instruction ultimately became the Bible.

How important is God's Word in your life? Of all the forms of God's communication, his written Word is the main way we can understand who God is, who we are, and what's going on in the world around us.

The Bible isn't just a book; it's God's living Word that can change us from the inside out. But don't just take my word for it. See for yourself.

> **THE BIBLE ISN'T JUST A BOOK; IT'S GOD'S LIVING WORD THAT CAN CHANGE US FROM THE INSIDE OUT.**

Apply the Bible's principles of forgiveness to your friendships and see if you aren't more peaceful. Apply the principles of honesty at school and see if you don't succeed. Apply the principles of honoring your parents and see if things don't improve at home.

Starting with Moses, the written Word changed the way God relates to his people. And it's been changing people in miraculous ways since then.

When we get to heaven, you can tell me how God's Word saved you from all kinds of problems and bad decisions and blessed you through all of his promises within it. You'll find me sitting with Moses at the street café just inside the pearly gates.

GOD'S PROMISES FOR YOU

When the Lord finished speaking to Moses on Mount Sinai, he gave him the two tablets of the covenant law, the tablets of stone inscribed by the finger of God.

EXODUS 31:18

Moses turned and went down the mountain with the two tablets of the covenant law in his hands. They were inscribed on both sides, front and back. The tablets were the work of God; the writing was the writing of God, engraved on the tablets.

EXODUS 32:15–16

I have not departed from his commands,
but have treasured his words more than daily food.

JOB 23:12 NLT

I have hidden your word in my heart,
that I might not sin against you.

PSALM 119:11 NLT

"This is what the Lord, the God of Israel, says: 'Write in a book all the words I have spoken to you.'"

JEREMIAH 30:2

Every part of Scripture is God-breathed and useful one way or another—showing us truth, exposing our rebellion, correcting our mistakes, training us to live God's way.

2 TIMOTHY 3:16 THE MESSAGE

God means what he says. What he says goes. His powerful Word is sharp as a surgeon's scalpel, cutting through everything, whether doubt or defense, laying us open to listen and obey. Nothing and no one is impervious to God's Word. We can't get away from it—no matter what.

HEBREWS 4:12–13 THE MESSAGE

THINK AND RESPOND

Why do you think God gave us his Word? For you, is the Bible mostly a book of facts, rules, or stories from a long time ago? Or is it a way to know God personally?

How often do you read the Bible? Would it be helpful to create a plan to read at a certain time of the day or through certain books of the Bible this year?

Read this statement again: "The Bible isn't just a book; it's God's living Word that transforms hearts and changes lives." How has it transformed your heart or changed your life?

What do you think it means that the words in the Bible are "God-breathed" (2 Timothy 3:16)? Does that change how you see the promises of God within it?

MY PROMISE TO GOD

I will spend time reading and studying the Bible. I believe that it is God-breathed and the key to understanding the larger story of my life, my faith, and the world. Through it, I will get to know more about God and his promises to me.

YOU ARE PART OF GOD'S FAMILY

We are heirs—heirs of God and co-heirs with Christ.

—ROMANS 8:17

Timothy Henry Gray's body was found under a Wyoming overpass two days after Christmas in 2012. There was no sign of foul play. No indication of a crime. A homeless 60-year-old cowboy who had died from the bitter cold, Gray was a victim of bad breaks and bad luck.

Except for this detail: he was supposed to inherit millions of dollars. Gray's great-grandfather was the founder of a small Nevada town you might have heard of: Las Vegas.

The man found dead under the railroad overpass wasn't poor after all. He was probably worth $19 million.[4] He just had no idea how rich he really was.

One of the most famous stories in the Bible has to do with inheritance. God had just rescued the Israelites from Egyptian captivity. He then led Moses and the people to the edge of the promised land.

"The Lord said to Moses, 'Send some men to explore the land of Canaan, which *I am giving* to the Israelites. From each ancestral tribe send one of its leaders'" (Numbers 13:1–2, emphasis mine).

God did not tell the Israelites to fight for the land. He told them he was giving it to them. Their fears screamed, "No way! Stay out! There are giants in the land." God's promise said, "The land is yours. The victory is yours. Take it." But they didn't. It was a bad decision that led to forty years of wandering in the wilderness.

Upon the death of Moses, Joshua became the leader of a new generation of people, and God reissued the promised land offer: "Moses my servant is dead. Now then, you and all these people, get ready to cross the Jordan River into the land I am about to give to them—to the Israelites. I will give you every place where you set your foot, as I promised Moses" (Joshua 1:2–3).

Joshua didn't "take the land" in his own strength. He "took

God at his word" and proceeded from there. He took the land, for sure. But he did so because he trusted God's promise.

The Israelites still had big problems to overcome. The Jordan River was wide. The Jericho walls were high. The evil inhabitants of Canaan wouldn't give up without a fight. Still, Joshua led the Israelites to cross the Jordan, brought down the walls of Jericho, and defeated the thirty-one enemy kings. Every time he faced a challenge, he did so with faith because he trusted God.

What if you did the same?

You may face a wall of fear and confusion. But then you remember: you are a child of God. His perfect love casts out fear. And you move forward.

> **GOD WILL PROVIDE WHAT YOU NEED TO FACE THE CHALLENGES OF LIFE.**

Is that to say that all your challenges will disappear? They didn't for Joshua. He fought for seven years! But he knew more victory than defeat.

So can you. It comes down to a simple decision to remember that your Father has an amazing inheritance reserved for you. He will provide what you need to face the challenges of life.

GOD'S PROMISES FOR YOU

Yours, O Lord, is the greatness, the power, the glory, the victory, and the majesty. Everything in the heavens and on earth is yours, O Lord, and this is your kingdom. We adore you as the one who is over all things.

1 CHRONICLES 29:11–12 NLT

"Only ask, and I will give you the nations as your inheritance,
the whole earth as your possession."

PSALM 2:8 NLT

The lowly will possess the land
and will live in peace and prosperity.

PSALM 37:11 NLT

This resurrection life you received from God is not a timid, grave-tending life. It's adventurously expectant, greeting God with a childlike "What's next, Papa?" God's Spirit touches our spirits and confirms who we really are. We know who he is, and we know who we are: Father and children. And we know we are going to get what's coming to us—an unbelievable inheritance!

ROMANS 8:15–17 THE MESSAGE

No eye has seen, no ear has heard,
and no mind has imagined
what God has prepared
for those who love him.

1 CORINTHIANS 2:9 NLT

We have a priceless inheritance—an inheritance that is kept in heaven for you, pure and undefiled, beyond the reach of change and decay.

1 PETER 1:4 NLT

THINK AND RESPOND

What attitude stopped the Israelites from entering the promised land for forty years? How do our actions sometimes delay the timing of God's gifts?

The Bible says Joshua and his followers received the promised land because God gave it to them. What promise is God ready to give you if you'd trust him for the outcome?

In Psalm 2:8, God said, "Only ask, and I will give you the nations as your inheritance, the whole earth as your possession" (NLT). That's a huge promise. As a child of the Father, what dreams and needs are you trusting God to meet?

Have you forgotten how rich you are as a child of God? How will remembering this promise take away fear and worry about your future?

MY PROMISE TO GOD

As God's heir and co-heir with Jesus, I will trust that he always has plenty of resources to meet my needs. No matter how hard life may seem, I will remember I am a child of God and am rich in his love, his promises, and his provisions.

GOD STRENGTHENS YOU

When the angel of the Lord appeared to Gideon, he said, "The Lord is with you, mighty warrior."

—JUDGES 6:12

If you were to open the mighty Mustangs yearbook from my freshman year of high school, I would have you take a good look at the freshman basketball team. Not the varsity or junior varsity team, but the ninth grade team. You would find two photos: one of the first string and one of the second string. I was on the second string . . . sort of.

The B-team had twelve players but only ten uniforms, which meant two of us didn't get to dress out. I was a decent height but had the coordination of a rhinoceros, so I didn't make the cut. The other no-uniform kid had thick glasses and a thicker waist. At least he had an excuse. So in the school picture, I wore jeans.

I didn't want to go to the photo shoot and have a memory of this moment. But just like I didn't know how to pick-and-roll on the court, I didn't know how to sneak out of the gym. My place as basketball nobody was documented for the ages.

GOD USES COMMON PEOPLE FOR UNCOMMON WORKS.

It was a Gideon moment. Do you remember Gideon's story in the Old Testament?

When God recruited him to help save Israel, Gideon's response was pretty weak. "Pardon me, my lord," Gideon replied, "but how can I save Israel? My clan is the weakest in Manasseh, and I am the least in my family" (Judges 6:15).

In other words, he claimed to be a wimp from a family of wimps. Yet God uses common people for uncommon works.

Special has nothing to do with how you look, your grade-point average, or what you can or can't do. *Special* has everything to do with the fact that you were created by the Master of the universe.

One of the biggest lies of the devil is that God only uses

special people. And like all lies of the devil, this one is based on a half-truth. God does use special people. Yet, they are special *because* God uses them.

Consider how he used Gideon's army. First, God sent home 95 percent of the troops to show the battle would be won in his strength. Then he revealed their coming victory by letting Gideon overhear the dream of a soldier in the enemy's camp.

"When Gideon heard the dream and its interpretation, he bowed down and worshiped. He returned to the camp of Israel and called out, 'Get up! The LORD has given the Midianite camp into your hands'" (Judges 7:15).

At first, matters seemed to be getting worse, not better. Can you relate? If so, Gideon is your new hero. He was inexperienced, his army was small, but his God was great.

Through their victory, Gideon learned what God wants us to learn: all we need is the presence of God. He is enough. We don't need a large army. We don't need endless resources. His presence tilts the scales in our favor.

We may not understand God's ways and, like Gideon, we may have questions. But let that promise find a permanent place in your heart, and remember: God will strengthen you.

GOD'S PROMISES FOR YOU

"Have I not commanded you? Be strong and courageous. Do not be afraid; do not be discouraged, for the LORD your God will be with you wherever you go."

JOSHUA 1:9

Even though I walk
through the darkest valley,
I will fear no evil,
for you are with me;
your rod and your staff,
they comfort me.

PSALM 23:4

"Don't worry, because I am with you.
Don't be afraid, because I am your God.
I will make you strong and will help you;
I will support you with my right hand that saves you."

ISAIAH 41:10 NCV

"Teach these new disciples to obey all the commands I have given you. And be sure of this: I am with you always, even to the end of the age."

MATTHEW 28:20 NLT

God can point to us in all future ages as examples of the incredible wealth of his grace and kindness toward us, as shown in all he has done for us who are united with Christ Jesus. God saved you by his grace when you believed. And you can't take credit for this; it is a gift from God. Salvation is not a reward for the good things we have done, so none of us can boast about it.

EPHESIANS 2:7–9 NLT

God has said,

"I will never fail you.
I will never abandon you."

HEBREWS 13:5 NLT

THINK AND RESPOND

Describe a time when you felt weak or wimpy. Did you pretend to be strong and know all the answers? Or did you ask for help? Why did you respond in that way?

Being "special" has nothing to do with how you look, what you can do, or how smart you are and everything to do with the fact that you are God's creation. Is it easy or hard to see yourself as God's unique creation? Why?

When you try to do things in your own strength, you feel weak and alone. But when you face challenges with God, you have his presence and strength. In what areas of your life right now do you need God's strength?

How can you experience God's presence more at school and throughout your day?

MY PROMISE TO GOD

I will remember that God gives me strength. He created me uniquely for this time and place in history. No matter what I face, I am never alone because God is with me.

YOUR REDEEMER CHOSE YOU

The Lord will redeem those who serve him. No one who takes refuge in him will be condemned.

—PSALM 34:22 NLT

My big brother loved picking on me. Growing up, no day was complete unless he made me miserable. He'd trip me as I entered the room. He'd wrestle me to the floor and sit on my chest until I couldn't breathe. He taught me the meaning of the word *wedgie*. His first waking thought must have been, *How can I pick on Max?*

But one day something miraculous happened. Instead of picking on me, he picked me to play on his baseball team. Mom said he could go to the park as long as he let me tag along. He groaned but said okay. By the time we arrived, the park was packed with kids ready to play ball. I was the youngest and least skilled of anyone there.

When the two best players began to pick teams, I knew I would be picked last—especially since my brother was one of the captains. But a miracle happened! Along with the stories of the Red Sea parting and Lazarus coming back to life is the moment my brother chose me: "I take Max." I walked through the unpicked players and took my place next to my unexpected hero. I went from the back of the pack to the front of the line, all because he called my name.

My brother didn't pick me because I was good. He called my name for one reason and one reason only: he was my big brother. And on that day he decided to be a good big brother. Redeemers behave this way. They spot the kid brother at the back of the crowd and call his name. They snatch the vulnerable out of trouble and place them under their care.

You might say he chose to be my "kinsman-redeemer." Actually, you'd never say that. You've probably never heard that term. But it's a good one to know because God promised to be your kinsman-redeemer.

This is exactly what Boaz was for Ruth in the Bible. Boaz was a wealthy property owner. Ruth had lost everything. He had workers. She needed work. She soon found herself working in a field belonging to Boaz (Ruth 2:2–3). When Boaz saw her, he perked up. Maybe she was pretty. Maybe he had a heart for the needy. Perhaps Cupid fired an arrow into his heart. Regardless, Boaz protected and provided for Ruth with such kindness that she asked, "Why have I found such favor in your eyes that you notice me—a foreigner?" (Ruth 2:10).

YOU MIGHT SAY THAT JESUS IS THE PERFECT BIG BROTHER. WHEN HE SPOTS YOU ON THE FIELD, HE MAKES CERTAIN YOU HAVE A SPOT ON HIS TEAM.

Redeemers offer more than one-time assistance. They rescue, for sure, but they provide a home, a purpose, and a future. Your Redeemer is doing this for you! You might say that Jesus is the perfect big brother. When he spots you on the field, he makes certain you have a spot on his team.

I never asked my brother what motivated him that day on the baseball diamond. I'd like to think that he picked me because of my talent, but I know better. He picked me because that's what a good big brother does. I guess he took a cue from Jesus.

GOD'S PROMISES FOR YOU

Don't urge me to leave you or turn back from you. Where you go I will go, and where you stay I will stay. Your people will be my people and your God my God.

RUTH 1:16

Praise be to the LORD, who this day has not left you without a guardian-redeemer. May he become famous throughout Israel!

RUTH 4:14

The righteous person may have many troubles,
but the LORD delivers him from them all.

PSALM 34:19

They remembered that God was their Rock,
that God Most High was their Redeemer.

PSALM 78:35

This is what the LORD says—
your Redeemer, the Holy One of Israel:
"I am the LORD your God,
who teaches you what is best for you,
who directs you in the way you should go."

ISAIAH 48:17

He has rescued us from the dominion of darkness and brought us into the kingdom of the Son He loves, in whom we have redemption, the forgiveness of sins.

COLOSSIANS 1:13-14

THINK AND RESPOND

Have you heard the term *kinsman-redeemer* before? How would you define this phrase in your own words? What do you like most about it?

Boaz protected and provided for Ruth with incredible kindness. Have you ever had a person like Boaz in your life? Describe the situation.

Have you ever come to the rescue of someone in need like Boaz did? What was that like for your heart—and for the person who received your help?

Redeemers offer more than one-time assistance. They rescue, for sure, but then they provide a home, a purpose, and a future for the one they rescued. How does Jesus do this for you?

MY PROMISE TO GOD

I will remember that Jesus is more than my rescuer—he is also my Redeemer. He provides for my needs and protects me from harm. I will trust him as my ultimate kinsman-redeemer.

GOD IS BIGGER THAN ANY GIANT

The battle is the LORD's.

—1 SAMUEL 17:47

The Philistines were warriors who were ready for battle. They had thirty thousand iron chariots and six thousand horsemen. And their MVP (Most Valuable Philistine) was Goliath. This champion warrior stood more than nine feet tall, wore 125 pounds of armor, and twice daily double-dog dared the Israelites to come fight him.

"This day I defy the armies of Israel! Give me a man and let us fight each other" (1 Samuel 17:10).

He was the undisputed bully of the valley: taunting, teasing. The giant had one goal; to suck the energy out of the Hebrew people. Eighty different times the Israelites ran from Goliath's challenges.

What giant strikes fear in you? Maybe it's a class that seems impossible to pass. Maybe it's being bullied at school. No one has to tell you that this life is a battle. But maybe you need a reminder that the battle is the Lord's.

David's story is a good one to remember. We know more about him than almost anyone in the Bible. It dedicates sixty-six chapters to his story, more than anyone other than Jesus. The New Testament mentions his name fifty-nine times!

By the time David arrived on the battle scene to bring his brothers food, the Israelite army had all but given up. David couldn't believe it. He stood up to the giant, calling Goliath—in today's language—a dirty, rotten scoundrel.

"What will be done for the man who kills this Philistine and removes this disgrace from Israel? Who is this uncircumcised Philistine that he should defy the armies of the living God?" (1 Samuel 17:26).

When the Israelite army saw Goliath, they focused on the

threat. When David saw Goliath, he focused on God. He went on to tell Goliath:

> You come against me with sword and spear and javelin, but I come against you in the name of the LORD Almighty, the God of the armies of Israel, whom you have defied. This day the LORD will deliver you into my hands, and I'll strike you down and cut off your head. This very day I will give the carcasses of the Philistine army to the birds and the wild animals, and the whole world will know that there is a God in Israel. All those gathered here will know that it is not by sword or spear that the LORD saves; for the battle is the LORD's, and he will give all of you into our hands. (1 Samuel 17:45–47)

He filtered his courage through God! The secret is remembering, "Our God will fight for us!" (Nehemiah 4:20).

YOU AREN'T ALONE IN YOUR STRUGGLES.

Lay claim to this great and powerful promise. It's not just you and Goliath. You aren't alone in your struggles. The next time you hear the bully of the valley snort and strut, remind yourself and him: "This battle is the LORD's."

GOD'S PROMISES FOR YOU

Our God will fight for us!

NEHEMIAH 4:20

You have given me your shield of victory.
Your right hand supports me;
your help has made me great.

PSALM 18:35 NLT

Some trust in chariots, others in horses,
but we trust the LORD our God.
They are overwhelmed and defeated,
but we march forward and win.

PSALM 20:7–8 NCV

When I walk into the thick of trouble,
keep me alive in the angry turmoil.
With one hand
strike my foes,
With your other hand
save me.

PSALM 138:7 THE MESSAGE

He grants a treasure of common sense to the honest.
He is a shield to those who walk with integrity.

PROVERBS 2:7 NLT

No, in all these things we are more than conquerors through him who loved us.

ROMANS 8:37

Put on every piece of God's armor so you will be able to resist the enemy in the time of evil. Then after the battle you will still be standing firm.

EPHESIANS 6:13 NLT

THINK AND RESPOND

What giant problems are you facing right now? Why do these issues seem so huge?

Have your eyes been more focused on the "giant" or on God? How would your situation improve if you focused on God's strength rather than the size of your problem?

It's easy to feel alone in your battles. But in 1 Samuel 17, David said that the battle belongs to the Lord. How would remembering this take the pressure off you?

David showed great courage when facing Goliath. He based that courage in God's strength rather than his. Describe a time when you were brave because you knew God was protecting you.

MY PROMISE TO GOD

I will face my battles in the name and in the strength of the mighty Lord. Rather than be distracted or intimidated by the giants that come against me, I will keep my eyes on God, knowing the battle belongs to him.

YOUR PRAYERS MATTER TO GOD

When a believing person prays, great things happen.

—JAMES 5:16 NCV

If you've ever wondered if your prayers really matter to God, the Old Testament prophet Elijah would like a word with you.

But since he lived eight hundred years before the birth of Jesus, we'll have to look back at his experience during one of the darkest times in Israel's history. The leaders were corrupt, and the hearts of the people were cold. Worse, there was a growing sense that idols could answer prayers better than God.

So Elijah called for a showdown: the true God of Israel against Baal, the false god to whom the people looked for rain and fertile fields. James 5:17 tells us, "Elijah was a human being just like us. He prayed that it would not rain, and it did not rain on the land for three and a half years!" (NCV).

What happened is one of the greatest stories in the Bible. After years of drought, Elijah told the prophets of Baal: "You get a bull; I'll get a bull. You build an altar of wood; I'll build an altar of wood. You ask your god to send fire; I'll ask my God to send fire. The God who answers by fire in the true God."

The prophets of Baal agreed and went first. They shouted for hours for Baal to send fire but nothing happened. Finally, Elijah asked for his turn. He poured four jugs of water over the wood altar three times. Then he prayed:

> "LORD, the God of Abraham, Isaac and Israel, let it be known today that you are God in Israel and that I am your servant and have done all these things at your command. Answer me, LORD, answer me, so these people will know that you, LORD, are God, and that you are turning their hearts back again." (1 Kings 18:36–37)

Note how quickly God answered his prayer.

> Then the fire of the LORD fell and burned up the sacrifice, the wood, the stones and the soil, and also licked up the water in the trench. When all the people saw this, they fell prostrate and cried, "The LORD—he is God! The LORD—he is God!" (1 Kings 18:38–39)

Notice that Elijah didn't ask God to send fire. God saw Elijah's heart, and pow! He set the altar ablaze.

Elijah's example shows us that prayer is not the last resort; it's the first step. God has power you've never seen, strength you've never known. He delighted in and answered Elijah's prayer. God delights in and will answer yours as well.

PRAYER IS NOT THE LAST RESORT; IT'S THE FIRST STEP.

But why? you may wonder. *Why would my prayers matter?*

Simple. Your prayers matter to God because you matter to God. You aren't just anybody; you are his child.

GOD'S PROMISES FOR YOU

> GOD's there, listening for all who pray,
> for all who pray and mean it.

PSALM 145:18 THE MESSAGE

"When you pray, you should go into your room and close the door and pray to your Father who cannot be seen. Your Father can see what is done in secret, and he will reward you. And when you pray, don't be like those people who don't know God. They continue saying things that mean nothing, thinking that God will hear them because of their many words. Don't be like them, because your Father knows the things you need before you ask him."

MATTHEW 6:6–8 NCV

"When two of you get together on anything at all on earth and make a prayer of it, my Father in heaven goes into action."

MATTHEW 18:19 THE MESSAGE

"Don't bargain with God. Be direct. Ask for what you need. This is not a cat-and-mouse, hide-and-seek game we're in."

LUKE 11:10 THE MESSAGE

The first thing I want you to do is pray. Pray every way you know how, for everyone you know. Pray especially for rulers and their governments to rule well so we can be quietly about our business of living simply, in humble contemplation.

1 TIMOTHY 2:1–2 THE MESSAGE

Let us then approach God's throne of grace with confidence, so that we may receive mercy and find grace to help us in our time of need.

HEBREWS 4:16

This is the confidence we have in approaching God: that if we ask anything according to his will, he hears us.

1 JOHN 5:14

THINK AND RESPOND

James 5:16 says, "When a believing person prays, great things happen" (NCV). Is it easy for you to believe this, or are you skeptical of the power of prayer? Why?

Do you see praying as talking to God in conversation rather than making formal requests and hoping they are answered? Which approach sounds better?

When is it hardest to pray? Why is that?

God may answer your prayers in unexpected ways. How does that make you feel?

MY PROMISE TO GOD

I will make prayer a priority because my prayers matter to God. I will trust that he knows the best way to answer my prayers. When times get tough, I will remember that I'm never without hope because I can always talk to him.

GOD HELPS THE HUMBLE

God opposes the proud
But gives grace to the humble.

—1 PETER 5:5 NLT

Have you heard the story of the boy who received the Most Humble badge but then had it taken away because he wore it? Humility is tricky because once you think you have it, you've probably lost it.

Being humble means you don't think too highly of yourself. Rather than being a know-it-all, you know all too well how much you need God and others. The Bible describes humility as the opposite of pride. And it's a big deal to God.

God gave us this amazing promise: "God opposes the proud but gives grace to the humble" (1 Peter 5:5 NLT). The Bible's most dramatic example of this promise occurs in the book of Daniel with the story of King Nebuchadnezzar. This power-hungry king overthrew Jerusalem in 609 BC and had a ninety-foot tall golden statue built in his honor. You might remember Nebuchadnezzar's fury when Shadrach, Meshach, and Abednego wouldn't bow to his statue. He had a furnace heated seven times hotter than its normal level and threw the men into the fire. When they came out unharmed, Nebuchadnezzar was amazed but refused to humble himself.

RATHER THAN BEING A KNOW-IT-ALL, YOU KNOW ALL TOO WELL HOW MUCH YOU NEED GOD AND OTHERS.

Years passed. Nebuchadnezzar was enjoying a time of peace and prosperity. His enemies were held at bay. His wealth was secure. Yet in the midst of this, Nebuchadnezzar had a strange dream that neither he nor his servants could understand. So he asked Daniel to explain it.

Daniel listened to the king's dream and gulped. God revealed to Daniel this warning for Nebuchadnezzar: humble yourself before it's too late.

Yet Nebuchadnezzar refused to repent. God gave the king another year to climb down from his pompous throne. But he never did.

> Even as the words were on his lips, a voice came from heaven, "This is what is decreed for you, King Nebuchadnezzar: Your royal authority has been taken from you. You will be driven away from people and will live with the wild animals; you will eat grass like the ox." (Daniel 4:31–32)

When the mighty fall, the fall is mighty. One minute Nebuchadnezzar thought he ran the world; the next he lived like a wild beast. And we are left with a lesson: God hates pride.

Pride comes at a high price. Don't pay it. Choose instead to stand on the offer of grace. "God opposes the proud but gives grace to the humble" (1 Peter 5:5 NLT).

To the degree God hates arrogance, he loves humility. Isn't it easy to see why? Humility is happy to do what pride will not. The humble heart is quick to acknowledge the need for God, eager to confess sin, willing to kneel before heaven's mighty hand.

Those who walk in pride God is able to humble. But those who walk in humility God is able to use.

GOD'S PROMISES FOR YOU

> Though the LORD is supreme,
> he takes care of those who are humble,
> but he stays away from the proud.

PSALM 138:6 NCV

I hate pride and arrogance.

PROVERBS 8:13

Do you see a person wise in their own eyes?
There is more hope for a fool than for them.

PROVERBS 26:12

Don't praise yourself; let others do it!

PROVERBS 27:2 TLB

The LORD has told you what is good,
and this is what he requires of you:
to do what is right, to love mercy,
and to walk humbly with your God.

MICAH 6:8 NLT

Don't think you are better than you really are. Be honest in your evaluation of yourselves, measuring yourselves by the faith God has given us.

ROMANS 12:3 NLT

In humility value others above yourselves.

PHILIPPIANS 2:3

Humble yourselves before the Lord, and he will lift you up.

JAMES 4:10

THINK AND RESPOND

When are you most tempted to brag about what you do well? Why?

Why do you think God hates pride and arrogance? What is his motive in encouraging you to be humble?

How does pride hurt your relationships with others? How does pride hurt your relationship with God?

In what areas of your life can you use more humility? Be specific.

MY PROMISE TO GOD

I will strive to be humble rather than prideful. I realize I don't have all the answers to life's problems, so I will humble myself before God. He will lift me up in the right ways at the right times.

YOU CAN TRUST GOD FOR THE OUTCOME

We know that in all things God works for the good of those who love him, who have been called according to his purpose.

—ROMANS 8:28

Have I told you about the day I nearly fell out of the sky?

A while back I decided to take flying lessons. And within twenty or so hours of instruction, I can honestly say I succeeded. I could take off. I could turn right and left, go higher and lower. I knew how to fly a plane.

What I didn't know was how to *land* a plane.

On the day I nearly fell from the sky, I had completed a lesson and was riding in the back seat when my instructor, Hank, said, "I'm about to be sick. I've got to put this plane down. I'm not able to fly." Those are words you never want to hear a pilot say. If Hank passed out, I couldn't reach the controls from the back seat. I couldn't radio for help. I couldn't fly the plane. Not to mention I didn't yet know how to land a plane. I was totally helpless.

Ever been there? Not in a plane, but in your life? If so, you'll relate to Esther. She was a young Jewish woman living in the Persian Empire around the fifth century BC. The villain of this story is Haman (whose name sounds a lot like *hangman*). He hated the Jewish people living there, so he convinced King Xerxes that they were bad people who needed to be killed. The king agreed and set in motion a plan that no one could reverse later—not even him.

ESTHER TOOK A STEP OF FAITH, AND GOD BLESSED HER OBEDIENCE. HE'LL DO THE SAME FOR YOU.

Esther and her uncle Mordecai were among the people who would die. But then God set in motion a series of miraculous events in which Esther went from being unknown to being crowned King Xerxes's queen. The king had no idea Esther was Jewish, or he never would have married her. Yet Esther had bigger concerns. Her people would soon be killed. Mordecai begged his niece to ask the king for mercy before it was too late.

Esther reminded Mordecai that even the queen couldn't just walk up to the king. She had to be invited, or she could lose her life.

Mordecai responded with a speech worthy of a Hollywood movie:

> Do not think that because you are in the king's house you alone of all the Jews will escape. For if you remain silent at this time, relief and deliverance for the Jews will arise from another place, but you and your father's family will perish. And who knows but that you have come to your royal position for such a time as this? (Esther 4:13–14)

Mordecai was certain the Jewish people would be helped. At question was not God's plan, but Esther's role in it. She made her choice: "I will go to the king, even though it is against the law. And if I perish, I perish" (Esther 4:16). She did what was right. She took a step of faith, and God blessed her obedience. He'll do the same for you.

By the way, as you've likely guessed, the plane did land safely, and we made it home. God promises that he will get you home as well.

GOD'S PROMISES FOR YOU

> Turn from evil and do good;
> seek peace and pursue it.
>
> **PSALM 34:14**

Trust [God] absolutely, people;
lay your lives on the line for him.

PSALM 62:8 THE MESSAGE

Trust the LORD with all your heart,
and don't depend on your own understanding.
Remember the LORD in all you do,
and he will give you success.

PROVERBS 3:5–6 NCV

We may throw the dice,
but the LORD determines how they fall.

PROVERBS 16:33 NLT

"Learn to do good.
Work for justice.
Help the down-and-out.
Stand up for the homeless.
Go to bat for the defenseless."

ISAIAH 1:17 THE MESSAGE

God, who got you started in this spiritual adventure, shares with us the life of his Son and our Master Jesus. He will never give up on you. Never forget that.

1 CORINTHIANS 1:9 THE MESSAGE

Let us not become weary in doing good, for at the proper time we will reap a harvest if we do not give up.

GALATIANS 6:9

THINK AND RESPOND

Have you ever stood up for what was right even though it came at a great cost to you? What was the end result? How did God protect you?

Do you sense that you are your age at this particular time in the history of the world for a great purpose? How will your school, your family, your church, or your community be different because of your presence?

God blesses your obedience after you step out in faith. In what area of your life do you need to stop waiting and step forward in faith? What is holding you back?

The Bible says in all things God works for the good of those who love him (Romans 8:28). Sometimes that process takes longer than you want. What situation are you still waiting for God to redeem for good? Write it down, and then talk to him about it.

MY PROMISE TO GOD

I will do what is right and trust God for the outcome. Even when I'm not sure what may happen, I will step out in faith and remember that God is working things out for my good.

THE BEST IS YET TO COME

"The glory of this present house will be greater than the glory of the former house," says the LORD Almighty.

—HAGGAI 2:9

The Bible is full of stories of people who made bad decisions and veered off track. The prodigal son wasted his inheritance. When he was dead broke, he had to feed pigs to make ends meet. The hourly wage must have stunk as bad as the pigs. The Old Testament prophet Jonah didn't want to help out a bunch of foreigners he didn't like, so he ran. God put him in a three-day timeout in the belly of a whale.

God can use what looks like setbacks to get our attention and help us get back on track. In God's plan, the future is always brighter than what came before. That's not positive thinking. It's one of God's most powerful promises.

The Bible says it this way: "The glory of this present house will be greater than the glory of the former house" (Haggai 2:9). With God, what's coming will always outshine what was.

We get a glimpse of what future glory looks like through the story of the rebuilding of God's temple. The Israelites had spent the last seventy years exiled from Jerusalem. Their city and the beloved temple were destroyed. Yet after seven decades, God set a plan in motion to rebuild his temple in Jerusalem by turning the heart of King Cyrus toward the Jews (Ezra 1).

WITH GOD, WHAT'S COMING WILL ALWAYS OUTSHINE WHAT WAS.

God prompted King Cyrus to give the exiles permission and resources to rebuild the temple. Why? The temple of ancient Israel served as a picture and proof of God's big thing: his desire to be close to his children.

The Jews rolled up the sleeves of their robes and got to work. Initially, they made God's priority their priority. But after a few years, they began to grow weary or distracted. One by one, little by little, person by person, they turned away from God's big thing and quit working on the temple. God's big thing became their small thing.

And like he let the prodigal son stink with the pigs and Jonah sink with the whale, God used a season of struggles to get the Jews' attention and turn their hearts back to God's house.

Military folks have a great term for this: an about face. A 180-degree turn. Change of direction. Change of intention. Change of heart. Repent. Turn. Redirect yourself.

Amazingly, the Jews did. The Lord stirred up the leadership and the people got to work on the house of God. They participated in the greatest work of heaven. God's word proved true. The glory of the latter was greater than the former.

God keeps his promises. What he said through Haggai has happened and will continue to happen. What he says to you will happen as well. Make his work your work, and the latter will be greater than the former. We simply need to focus on God's work—doing whatever he wants us to do right now.

It's not too late to start again.

GOD'S PROMISES FOR YOU

May the favor of the LORD our God rest on us;
establish the work of our hands for us—
yes, establish the work of our hands.

PSALM 90:17

Commit your actions to the LORD,
and your plans will succeed.

PROVERBS 16:3 NLT

"I know what I am planning for you," says the LORD. "I have good plans for you, not plans to hurt you. I will give you hope and a good future."

JEREMIAH 29:11 NCV

"Go up into the mountains and bring down timber and build my house."

HAGGAI 1:8

"I am with you," declares the LORD.

HAGGAI 1:13

The nations will walk by its light, and the kings of the earth will bring their splendor into it. On no day will its gates ever be shut, for there will be no night there. The glory and honor of the nations will be brought into it. Nothing impure will ever enter it, nor will anyone who does what is shameful or deceitful, but only those whose names are written in the Lamb's book of life.

REVELATION 21:24–27

THINK AND RESPOND

Is it difficult to think your future could be better? What is the main thing from your past that seems to get in the way of a better future?

God promises to make all things new (Revelation 21:5). What would you like for him to make new in your life now? Why?

What do you think about the location of God's temple and how that reflects his desire to dwell with his people? Does that give you new insight into how God wants to be actively involved in the details of your life?

When the Jews built the house of God, they participated in the greatest work of heaven. Through it, the glory of the latter was greater than the former. When you make his work your work, you will experience a brighter future as well. What is a possible project that God is inviting you to pursue with him and for his glory?

MY PROMISE TO GOD

I will make God's work my work. As I do so, I will participate with God in building a brilliant future that outshines the past.

THE POWER OF CHRIST IS IN YOU

It is God who works in you to will and to act in order to fulfill his good purpose.

—PHILIPPIANS 2:13

What if Mary were God's second choice to be Jesus' earthly mom? Might there have been another girl to whom the angel Gabriel went first? Could it be possible that the invitation was first offered to a girl named Hannah, Olivia, or Ruby?

"Who, me?" Mary could have said to Gabriel. "God wants to live inside of me?" She could have given a thousand reasons why it wouldn't work. *I'm too simple. Too little. Too common. Too poor. Too, well, I'm too human. Besides, since when does God go about moving in and living inside someone? Thanks, but no thanks. I'll keep my normal life.*

Was Mary God's Plan B? Who knows? But if someone heard the offer and refused the invitation, we can't be too harsh. It was a bold one. An angel revealed God's promise to her: "The Holy Spirit will come on you, and the power of the Most High will overshadow you. So the holy one to be born will be called the Son of God" (Luke 1:35).

GOD IS WORKING IN YOU! HE IS AT WORK TO HELP YOU WANT TO DO AND BE ABLE TO DO WHAT PLEASES HIM.

Mary was willing to believe the wildest of promises. Can we call it the promise of regeneration? A big word, for sure, but it describes this miracle, first seen in Mary—then offered to any who would follow in her steps. The Mary miracle is Christ in you.

That's what the Bible is getting at when it says, "It is God who works in you to will and to act in order to fulfill his good purpose" (Philippians 2:13). God is working in you! He is at work to help you want to do and be able to do what pleases him. An Old Testament verse says it this way:

> "I will give you a new heart and put a new spirit in you; I will remove from you your heart of stone and give you a heart of flesh. And I will put my Spirit in you and move you to follow my decrees and be careful to keep my laws. Then you will live in the land I gave your ancestors; you will be my people, and I will be your God." (Ezekiel 36:26–28)

God gives you an offer like the one he gave Mary—the supernatural presence of his Son in your life. Jesus lives in his children. Paul's prayer for the Ephesians was "that Christ may dwell in your hearts through faith" (Ephesians 3:17). What is the mystery of the gospel? "Christ in you, the hope of glory" (Colossians 1:27). John was clear: "The one who keeps God's commands lives in him, and he in them" (1 John 3:24).

Take note of the word *in*. Christ isn't just *near* you or *for* you or *with* you—he is longing to be *in* you. Christ grew in Mary until he came out. Christ will grow in you until he comes out in your speech, in your actions, in your decisions. He was a baby in her. He is a force in you.

Like Mary, you now get to share Christ with the world.

GOD'S PROMISES FOR YOU

"I will give you a new heart and put a new spirit in you."

EZEKIEL 36:26

I have reason to be enthusiastic about all Christ Jesus has done through me in my service to God.

ROMANS 15:17 NLT

I pray that out of his glorious riches he may strengthen you with power through his Spirit in your inner being, so that Christ may dwell in your hearts through faith.

EPHESIANS 3:16–17

This is the secret: Christ lives in you. This gives you assurance of sharing his glory.

COLOSSIANS 1:27 NLT

You accepted what we said as the very word of God—which, of course, it is. And this word continues to work in you who believe.

1 THESSALONIANS 2:13 NLT

The one who keeps God's commands lives in him, and he in them. And this is how we know that he lives in us: We know it by the Spirit he gave us.

1 JOHN 3:24

THINK AND RESPOND

Have you considered the faith and courage Mary had to say yes to God's invitation to carry and give birth to his Son? What fears or concerns do you think she had?

What does it mean to have "Christ in you" (Colossians 1:27)? How does that truth change who you are from the inside out?

When the Bible says, "It is God who works in you to will and to act in order to fulfill his good purpose" (Philippians 2:13), it means God helps you want to do and be able to do what pleases him. In what ways has God recently done this in your life?

Name several ways that you actively share Christ to those around you, whether you know them from school or sports or they're your family members.

MY PROMISE TO GOD

I welcome God's presence and work in my life. I know he lives in me. Through my words, choices, and actions, I will share Christ with those in my world.

GOD UNDERSTANDS YOU

Our high priest is able to understand our weaknesses. He was tempted in every way that we are, but he did not sin.

—HEBREWS 4:15 NCV

God gets you. He understands your pain, questions, tears, and fears. But how can an all-powerful God possibly understand our messy lives? He can because he became one of us. "The Word became flesh and made his dwelling among us" (John 1:14).

Had Jesus simply come down to earth in the form of a mighty being, we would respect him but never would draw near to him. After all, how could God understand what it means to be human?

HOW CAN AN ALL-POWERFUL GOD POSSIBLY UNDERSTAND OUR MESSY LIVES? HE CAN BECAUSE HE BECAME ONE OF US.

Had Jesus been biologically conceived with two earthly parents, we would feel comfortable around him, but would we want to worship him? After all, he would be no different than you and me.

But if Jesus was both—God and man at the same time—then we have the best of both worlds. He was fully human. He was fully divine. Because of the first, we relate to him. Because of the latter, we worship him. Here's how the Bible describes it:

> The Son is the image of the invisible God, the firstborn over all creation. For in him all things were created: things in heaven and on earth, visible and invisible, whether thrones or powers or rulers or authorities; all things have been created through him and for him. (Colossians 1:15–16)

Not one drop of divinity was lost in the change to humanity. Though Jesus appeared human, he was actually God. The star maker, for a time, built cabinets in Nazareth. "It was the Father's good pleasure for all the fullness to dwell in Him" (Colossians 1:19 NASB). But his power was—and is—absolute. You think the moon affects the tides? It does. But Christ runs the moon. You think the United States is a superpower? The United States has only the power Christ gives and nothing more. He has authority over everything. And he has had it forever.

Yet Jesus was willing for a time to become like us. He was born just like babies are born. His childhood was a common one. "Jesus grew in wisdom and stature, and in favor with God and man" (Luke 2:52). He knew the pain of sore muscles, the hurt of betrayal, and the joy of close friends.

Does this promise matter? If you ever wonder if the uncreated Creator can, in a million years, understand what you're going through, it does. Jesus is "able to understand our weaknesses" (Hebrews 4:15 NCV). The One who hears your prayers understands your pain. He never minimizes physical struggle. He had a human body.

Are you troubled in spirit? He was too (John 12:27). Are you anxious and overwhelmed? He was too (Matthew 26:38). Are you sad with grief? He was too (John 11:35). Have you ever prayed through tears? He did too (Hebrews 5:7).

Because Jesus is human, he understands you. Because he is divine, he can help you. He gets you.

GOD'S PROMISES FOR YOU

> God has surely listened
> and has heard my prayer.
>
> **PSALM 66:19**

Great is our Lord and mighty in power;
his understanding has no limit.

PSALM 147:5

What kind of man is this? Even the winds and the waves obey him!

MATTHEW 8:27

In the beginning the Word already existed.
The Word was with God,
and the Word was God.
He existed in the beginning with God.

JOHN 1:1–2 NLT

The Word became flesh and made his dwelling among us. We have seen his glory, the glory of the one and only Son, who came from the Father, full of grace and truth.

JOHN 1:14

The Son is the image of the invisible God, the firstborn over all creation. For in him all things were created: things in heaven and on earth, visible and invisible, whether thrones or powers or rulers or authorities; all things have been created through him and for him.

COLOSSIANS 1:15–16

God in all his fullness
was pleased to live in Christ.

COLOSSIANS 1:19 NLT

THINK AND RESPOND

Some people see Jesus mostly as a man who did some miracles. Others see him mostly as God who was pretending to be human during his time on earth. The Bible makes it clear he was both fully human and fully divine. Explain what that means in your own words.

What makes the specific way Jesus came to earth so special? How does his birth on earth impact the way he can relate to us?

Do you tend to view Jesus through his humanity or through his divinity? How does this affect your relationship with him?

You may think God can't relate to what you're going through, yet the One who hears our prayers understands your pain. What issues have you been keeping from God because you felt he didn't care or wouldn't get it?

MY PROMISE TO GOD

I celebrate how Jesus came to this world. He was fully human, so he knows how hard life can be. And he was fully divine, so he can heal my hurts. I will forever stay close to God, knowing he understands everything I feel and everything I need.

JESUS OFFERS LIVING WATER

"The water I give will become a spring of water gushing up inside that person, giving eternal life."

—JOHN 4:14 NCV

Some of the most incredible invitations are found in the pages of the Bible. You can't read about God without finding him issuing invitations. He invited Eve to marry Adam, the animals to enter the ark, David to be king, Mary to give birth to his Son, and the disciples to go from fishermen to fishers of men.

God is a God who invites. God is a God who calls. And God is a God who satisfies people's thirst. But his invitation is not just for a meal or a cup of water. It is for life.

John 4 tells us the story of a Samaritan woman Jesus encountered at the well. As a Samaritan woman, she knew the sting of racism and sexism. She'd been married to five men. She was an outcast. Yet when Jesus asked her for a cup of water to quench his thirst, he offered her an invitation to satisfy her soul: "The water I give will become a spring of water gushing up inside that person, giving eternal life" (v. 14 NCV).

The Samaritan woman was curious about Jesus' offer.

> The woman said to him, "Sir, give me this water so that I won't get thirsty and have to keep coming here to draw water."
>
> He told her, "Go, call your husband and come back." (vv. 15–16)

Her heart must have sunk. Here was a Jew who didn't care if she was a Samaritan. Here was a man who didn't look down on her as a woman. Here was the closest thing to gentleness she'd ever seen. And now he was asking her about what she was most ashamed of. Maybe she considered lying about it. Or she was tempted to change the subject. She likely just wanted to leave. Maybe she worried that Jesus' kindness would stop once the truth was revealed. But she stayed and told the truth: "I have no husband" (v. 17).

If you've ever worried that you've messed up too much or you're too far gone for Jesus' love and forgiveness, take note of his response to the Samaritan woman: Jesus offered no criticism. No anger. No look-at-the-mess-you've-made lecture. Just honesty with an invitation to live differently from that point forward.

Can you relate to the Samaritan woman? We know why she was avoiding people . . . because we do the same. We know what it's like to have no one sit by us at the cafeteria. We've wondered what it would be like to have just one good friend. We've trusted others with our heart and wondered if it's worth the pain to try again. And like the Samaritan woman, we've wondered where God is.

Her story answers these questions. It shows the length he will go to reach us right where we are. It shows that he can use us in spite of our past. And it shows how only he can fill our thirst. Nothing else works.

> **JESUS IS THE ONLY ONE WHO CAN SATISFY YOUR DEEPEST THIRST.**

Jesus' invitation to the woman at the well is his invitation to you. He's the only one who can satisfy your deepest thirst. And he does so with real living-water life.

Go ahead, take a drink.

GOD'S PROMISES FOR YOU

You, God, are my God,
earnestly I seek you;
I thirst for you,

my whole being longs for you,
in a dry and parched land
where there is no water.

PSALM 63:1

With joy you will draw water
from the wells of salvation.

ISAIAH 12:3

"I will pour out water for the thirsty land
and make streams flow on dry land.
I will pour out my Spirit into your children
and my blessing on your descendants."

ISAIAH 44:3 NCV

"I will sprinkle clean water on you, and you will be clean. Your filth will be washed away, and you will no longer worship idols."

EZEKIEL 36:25 NLT

"If anyone believes in me, rivers of living water will flow out from that person's heart, as the Scripture says." Jesus was talking about the Holy Spirit. The Spirit had not yet been given, because Jesus had not yet been raised to glory. But later, those who believed in Jesus would receive the Spirit.

JOHN 7:38–39 NCV

The Lamb at the center of the throne
will be their shepherd;
'he will lead them to springs of living water.'
'And God will wipe away every tear from their eyes.'

REVELATION 7:17

THINK AND RESPOND

Have you tried to fill your thirst with things other than God? What has been the result?

God doesn't keep a record of our wrongs, but sometimes we keep a list of how others have hurt us. Do you struggle with this? If so, why do you think this is?

When Jesus asked the woman at the well for a drink, what thoughts do you think were going through her head? Do you think she had any idea of how her life was about to change?

Has Jesus showed up in your life at a time and in a way you didn't expect? What happened, and how did the encounter change you?

MY PROMISE TO GOD

I will drink from the living water of Christ. I will look only to him to fill my thirst. I will say yes to his invitation, knowing his death and resurrection make me fully worthy of the call. As an adopted child of God, I never have to be thirsty again.

YOU MATTER IN GOD'S KINGDOM

"Seek first his kingdom and his righteousness, and all these things will be given to you as well."

—MATTHEW 6:33

I always thought it would be great to know the kid of a king. Maybe he or she could answer some of these questions: *Have you ever seen the king in pajamas? Does he let ever let you sit on the throne? Have you worn his crown when he wasn't looking?*

If only I knew a royal family. Then I remembered that I sort of did. My hometown knew nothing of crowns and castles, but we were all about football. Every Friday night our small town would gather in the stadium to cheer for the mighty Mustangs.

And since football reigned supreme, the head coach was King Leach. When he shouted "jump," we turned into human grasshoppers. But my buddy Jim was also his son. I remember the two of them, coach and son, leaving practice together: laughing, tossing a ball as they walked, headed toward the same dinner table.

Jim had the coach for a dad. But you and I have so much more than a coach for our dad. With God, we have the most powerful King in the universe as our Father.

The greatest of the kingdom secrets is not just that a kingdom exists or that the kingdom has a King—but that the King is your Father. That's why Jesus taught us to pray "Our Father in heaven, hallowed be your name, your kingdom come" (Matthew 6:9–10).

WITH GOD, WE HAVE THE MOST POWERFUL KING IN THE UNIVERSE AS OUR FATHER.

When your father is king, everything changes. If some fearless force rules from behind a castle wall, you have a king and nothing more. But if the king is the man who butters your bread and tucks you in and locks the door at night, you have more than a king; you have a reason to smile. You know the king's heart, and the king knows your name. He listens when you call. He cares when you hurt. And he's ready to rescue you.

Our King loves us, but his kingdom is not about us. We might assume it is . . . after all, aren't we children of the King? The kingdom exists to make us happy, to fill us, to fulfill us, to fix us. The kingdom is about us, right?

No, it's about God. We benefit from being a part of his kingdom, no doubt. But we are not the heroes of the story. God is. He invites us to be a part of his kingdom. There is only one condition. The kingdom has one King. You and I are welcome to enter the throne room, but we have to surrender our crowns at the door.

In our society, the thought of kings and absolute rule makes us absolutely nervous. We prefer the idea of a democracy where everyone has an equal voice. Yet the Bible is clear that God is King. The entire creation, both humans and nature, answers to him. The Old Testament prophets looked to the arrival of an anointed King, a Messiah, one uniquely related to God to serve as the instrument of his rule. "Look, your king is coming to you. He is righteous and victorious, yet he is humble, riding on a donkey" (Zechariah 9:9 NLT). At the arrival of Jesus, God-fearing Jews said: "'The time has come,' he said. 'The kingdom of God has come near'" (Mark 1:15).

God's kingdom is more about changing hearts than charging knights. And you have a key role to play. Best of all, you already know the King. He is your Father.

GOD'S PROMISES FOR YOU

You alone are God of all the kingdoms of the earth. You alone created the heavens and the earth.

ISAIAH 37:16 NLT

God's rule is forever,
and his kingdom continues for all time.

DANIEL 4:34 NCV

Our Father in heaven,
may your name be kept holy.
May your Kingdom come soon.
May your will be done on earth,
as it is in heaven.

MATTHEW 6:9–10 NLT

"The time has come," [Jesus] said. "The kingdom of God has come near. Repent and believe the good news!"

MARK 1:15

"I must preach the Good News of the Kingdom of God in other towns, too, because that is why I was sent."

LUKE 4:43 NLT

Jesus said, "What is God's kingdom like? What can I compare it with? It is like a mustard seed that a man plants in his garden. The seed grows and becomes a tree, and the wild birds build nests in its branches."

LUKE 13:18–19 NCV

Jesus replied, "The Kingdom of God can't be detected by visible signs. You won't be able to say, 'Here it is!' or 'It's over there!' For the Kingdom of God is already among you."

LUKE 17:20–21 NLT

THINK AND RESPOND

Write your thoughts to this quote from the chapter: *The greatest of the kingdom secrets is not just that a kingdom exists or that the kingdom has a King—but that the King is your Father.*

If you've grown up in a democracy, is it hard to think about living in a kingdom led by the absolute rule of a King? Does it help knowing that King is God?

Our King loves us, but his kingdom is not about us. It's about God. Yet he generously gives each of us a role to play in his story. How does it feel to have a key role to play?

As the King's son or daughter, you help bring God's kingdom into the world through your prayers and actions. List a few ways you are doing this.

MY PROMISE TO GOD

I am a citizen of God's kingdom. He is my King and also my Father. I will help introduce others to his kingdom and worship him with all my heart, strength, and mind.

JESUS CALMS YOUR STORMS

Jesus . . . is at the right hand of God
and is also interceding for us.

—ROMANS 8:34

Storms aren't just in the sky. Some storms rage into our lives out of nowhere and mess everything up. A friend lets you down. A grade goes way down. Your fears go up. These storms hit fast and hard.

You might think now that we belong to God, we should get a pass on bad news, bad hair days, and bad grades. After all, to follow Jesus is to live a storm-free life, right? (Are you laughing yet?) The truth of the matter is this: life comes with storms. Jesus assured us, "In this world you will have trouble" (John 16:33).

In Matthew 14, the disciples were on a storm-tossed sea because Jesus told them to be there. "Jesus made the disciples get into the boat" (v. 22). The disciples launched the boat as Jesus instructed only to sail headfirst into chaos.

When they had rowed "three or four miles" (John 6:19), the storm hit. Evening became night, night became windy and rainy, and before long their boat was riding the raging roller coaster of the Galilean sea.

Let's climb into the boat with them. Look into their rain-splattered faces. What do you see? Fear, for sure. Doubt? Absolutely. You may even hear a question shouted over the wind. "Anyone know where Jesus is?"

The question is not recorded in the text, but it was surely asked. When a ferocious storm pounced on obedient disciples, where in the world was Jesus?

The answer is clear and surprising: praying.

Jesus "went up on a mountainside by himself to pray" (Matthew 14:23). After he'd served all day, he prayed all night. He felt the powerful winds and the skin-stinging rain. He, too, was in the storm, but still he prayed.

Think about this promise. Jesus, right now, at this moment,

in the midst of your storm, is praying for you. The King of the universe is speaking on your behalf. He is calling out to the heavenly Father. He is urging the help of the Holy Spirit. He is asking for a special blessing to be sent your way. You do not fight the wind and waves alone. It's not up to you to find a solution.

"Where is Jesus?" the disciples may have asked.

Where is Jesus? you may ask in the middle of your storm.

He is in the presence of God, praying for us.

JESUS, RIGHT NOW, AT THIS MOMENT, IN THE MIDST OF YOUR STORM, IS PRAYING FOR YOU.

Unshakable hope is the firstborn offspring of this promise. We'd like to know the future, but we don't. We long to see the road ahead, but we can't. We'd prefer to have every question answered, but instead Jesus simply said, "I will pray you through the storm."

Are the prayers of Jesus answered? Of course. Will you make it through this storm? I think you know the answer.

GOD'S PROMISES FOR YOU

Be strong and take heart,
all you who hope in the LORD.

PSALM 31:24

He stilled the storm to a whisper;
the waves of the sea were hushed.

PSALM 107:29

The disciples went and woke him, saying, "Master, Master, we're going to drown!" He got up and rebuked the wind and the raging waters; the storm subsided, and all was calm.

LUKE 8:24

"I have told you these things, so that in me you may have peace. In this world you will have trouble. But take heart! I have overcome the world."

JOHN 16:33

He is able to save completely those who come to God through him, because he always lives to intercede for them.

HEBREWS 7:25

"You have persevered and have endured hardships for my name, and have not grown weary."

REVELATION 2:3

THINK AND RESPOND

Does it seem unfair that as Christians we have to still go through hard times? Knowing that even Jesus had to face storms, does that change your opinion?

What current storm (difficult circumstances) are you facing? What are you most afraid might happen?

Where do you think Jesus is during this situation? Do you think he is busy doing other things or actively helping you through it?

Did you realize that during hard times Jesus is praying for you? How does that make you feel?

MY PROMISE TO GOD

I know hard times will come my way. In the middle of these storms, I will not lose hope because I know that Jesus is praying for me, is with me, and will see me through no matter what situation I may face.

YOU'RE COMPLETELY FORGIVEN

There is now no condemnation for
those who are in Christ Jesus.

—ROMANS 8:1

Sometime back I took up swimming for exercise. Over the weeks I went from a tadpole to a small frog. I'm not much to look at, but I can get up and down the lane. In fact, I started to feel pretty good about my progress.

So good, in fact, that when Olympian Josh Davis invited me to swim with him, I accepted. What you might not know is that Josh was a swimmer in two Summer Olympic Games in which he won three gold medals and two silver medals. Half of his warm-up is my entire workout. He is as comfortable in a swimming lane as most of us are in a cafeteria lane.

So when he offered to give me some pointers, I jumped in the pool. (A pool, incidentally, that bears the name Josh Davis Natatorium.) With Josh in his lane and me next to him in mine, he suggested, "Let's swim two laps and let's see how fast you go." Off I went. I gave it all I had. I was surprised at the finish to see that he had touched the wall only seconds before me. I felt pretty good about myself.

"Have you been here long?" I panted.

"Just a few seconds."

"You mean I finished only a few seconds behind you?"

"That's right."

But then Josh added, "There was one difference. While you swam two laps, I swam six." In that pool, I wasn't just a little behind. In that pool, I would never be able to catch up.

The gold standard of heaven puts us even more behind. God is holy; we are not. He is perfect; we are not. His character is flawless; ours is flawed.

What do we do? Give up? Lose hope? Quit trying? No one loved to answer that question more than the apostle Paul. His response? "There is now no condemnation for those who are in Christ Jesus" (Romans 8:1).

Paul described God's solution in three parts: Our sin is enough to sink us. God loves us too much to leave us. So he found a way to save us. He didn't decide sin was no big deal or that it didn't need to be paid for. God never compromises his standard. Too holy to overlook our sin and yet too loving to leave us in our sin, God did something radical. He placed our sin on his Son. "[Jesus] personally carried our sins in his body on the cross so that we can be dead to sin and live for what is right. By his wounds you are healed" (1 Peter 2:24 NLT).

OUR SIN IS ENOUGH TO SINK US. GOD LOVES US TOO MUCH TO LEAVE US. SO HE FOUND A WAY TO SAVE US.

This is God's grace. Gone is the fear of falling short! Gone is the pressure to prove yourself or hide from your sins. "God put the wrong on him who never did anything wrong, so we could be put right with God" (2 Corinthians 5:21 THE MESSAGE).

Don't miss that. You are right with God. Christ's death brought new life. Every obstacle that had separated—or could separate—you from God is gone. Could there be a better promise than that?

GOD'S PROMISES FOR YOU

If you, GOD, kept records on wrongdoings,
who would stand a chance?
As it turns out, forgiveness is your habit,
and that's why you're worshiped.

PSALM 130:3–4 THE MESSAGE

"Though your sins are like scarlet,
they shall be as white as snow;
though they are red as crimson,
they shall be like wool."

ISAIAH 1:18

Where is the god who can compare with you—
wiping the slate clean of guilt,
Turning a blind eye, a deaf ear,
to the past sins of your purged and precious people?
You don't nurse your anger and don't stay angry long,
for mercy is your specialty. That's what you love most.
And compassion is on its way to us.
You'll stamp out our wrongdoing.
You'll sink our sins to the bottom of the ocean.

MICAH 7:18–19 THE MESSAGE

This is my blood of the covenant, which is poured out for many for the forgiveness of sins.

MATTHEW 26:28

All have sinned and fall short of the glory of God.

ROMANS 3:23

God sacrificed Jesus on the altar of the world to clear that world of sin. Having faith in him sets us in the clear. God decided on this course of action in full view of the public—to set the world in the clear with himself through the sacrifice of Jesus, finally taking care of the sins he had so patiently endured. This is not only clear, but it's *now*—this is current history! God sets things right. He also makes it possible for us to live in his rightness.

ROMANS 3:25–26 THE MESSAGE

THINK AND RESPOND

Have you worried whether all your sins have been forgiven—even the ones no one knows about? Does God say he forgives only some sins or all of your sins? Why is this important?

Paul described God's grace toward our sins in three parts. Which of the three is hardest for you to believe?

God never compromises his standard. Too holy to overlook our sin and yet too loving to leave us in our sin, God did something radical. Explain what he did—and what the cost was to Jesus.

When you accept Jesus as your Savior, you are made right with God. How does it feel to know that all your sins—past, present, and future—are forgiven because of his payment on the cross?

MY PROMISE TO GOD

I find forgiveness because of what Jesus did for me on the cross. Through his sacrifice, the payment of my sins is complete. I will live each day knowing I have been made right with God.

DEATH ISN'T THE END

Death has been swallowed up in victory.

—1 CORINTHIANS 15:54

What if this life is as good as it gets? Sure, you've had some good times. But what if you never have a better day than what you've already had? What if your best moments were behind you? What if tomorrow were less than today, and today less than yesterday? If that were true, we would soon lose hope.

WE HAVE THE PROMISE OF AN ETERNITY WITH GOD THAT WILL FAR EXCEED OUR BEST MOMENTS ON EARTH.

But as believers in Jesus we have the promise of a better tomorrow. More than that, we have the promise of an eternity with God that will far exceed our best moments on earth.

"I am making everything new!" God announced (Revelation 21:5). This promise hinges on the resurrection of Christ. The Christian hope depends entirely upon the belief that Jesus died a physical death, vacated an actual grave, and ascended into heaven where he, at this moment, reigns as head of the church. The resurrection changed everything.

It was Sunday morning after the Friday crucifixion of Jesus. The sky was dark. The disciples had scattered. The Roman executioner may have been wondering about breakfast or his next day off, but he was not wondering about the guy he had nailed to a cross and pierced with a spear. Jesus was dead and buried. Yesterday's news, right?

Wrong.

> There was a violent earthquake, for an angel of the Lord came down from heaven and, going to the tomb, rolled back the stone and sat on it. His appearance was like lightning, and his clothes were white as snow. The guards were so afraid of him that they shook and became like dead men.

> The angel said to the women, "Do not be afraid, for I know that you are looking for Jesus, who was crucified. He is not here; he has risen, just as he said. Come and see the place where he lay." (Matthew 28:2–6)

Jesus was raised from the dead. And his resurrection is the preview and promise of ours. What God did for him, he will do for us. When we're young, anyone older than twenty-nine seems ancient (I won't tell you my age)! But one day we will all breathe our last breath on earth, as will everyone we love. And in every one of those moments, "Death is swallowed up in victory" (1 Corinthians 15:54 NLT).

The grave brings sorrow, for sure, but it doesn't need to bring hopelessness. The tomb could not contain Christ, and since Christ is in you, you will not long be in your tomb. "In keeping with his promise we are looking forward to a new heaven and a new earth, where righteousness dwells" (2 Peter 3:13).

Can I beg you to set your heart on this hope? "Since we are receiving a kingdom that cannot be shaken" (Hebrews 12:28), we can have a hope that won't be shaken. Set your heart and eyes on it.

Because this life isn't as good as it gets. With God, your future is guaranteed to be better than anything in your past. That's a promise.

GOD'S PROMISES FOR YOU

He said, "Jesus, remember me when you enter your kingdom." He said, "Don't worry, I will. Today you will join me in paradise."

LUKE 23:42–43 THE MESSAGE

Our old way of life was nailed to the cross with Christ, a decisive end to that sin-miserable life—no longer at sin's every beck and call! What we believe is this: If we get included in Christ's sin-conquering death, we also get included in his life-saving resurrection. We know that when Jesus was raised from the dead it was a signal of the end of death-as-the-end. Never again will death have the last word. When Jesus died, he took sin down with him, but alive he brings God down to us.

ROMANS 6:6–10 THE MESSAGE

Death has been swallowed up in victory.

1 CORINTHIANS 15:54

We do not give up. Our physical body is becoming older and weaker, but our spirit inside us is made new every day. We have small troubles for a while now, but they are helping us gain an eternal glory that is much greater than the troubles. We set our eyes not on what we see but on what we cannot see. What we see will last only a short time, but what we cannot see will last forever.

2 CORINTHIANS 4:16–18 NCV

We are eagerly waiting for him to return as our Savior. He will take our weak mortal bodies and change them into glorious bodies like his own, using the same power with which he will bring everything under his control.

PHILIPPIANS 3:20–21 NLT

He will wipe every tear from their eyes. There will be no more death or mourning or crying or pain, for the old order of things has passed away. He who was seated on the throne said, "I am making everything new!"

REVELATION 21:4–5

THINK AND RESPOND

Has someone close to you passed away? What was that experience like? How did it affect your view of death?

The Bible says, "We know that when Jesus was raised from the dead it was a signal of the end of death-as-the-end. Never again will death have the last word" (Romans 6:9 THE MESSAGE). How does this bring you hope when you face the loss of a family member or friend?

This isn't as good as it gets. How would it change your day today knowing your best days are still to come? Why?

What are you most excited about regarding God's promise to make all things new one day?

MY PROMISE TO GOD

I will not fear tomorrow. The resurrection of Jesus means that death is not the end of my story. I will live knowing that today is the beginning of a future beyond belief both here on earth and later in eternity.

JOY WILL COME SOON

Weeping may last through the night,
but joy comes with the morning.

—PSALM 30:5 NLT

Because God is exactly who he says he is, he offers hope to those who are sad and hurting. A pep talk might get you through a bad mood or a rough patch. But what about your parents' divorce or a debilitating accident? Does God have a word for the dark nights of the soul?

He does. The promise begins with this verse: "Weeping may last through the night, but joy comes with the morning" (Psalm 30:5 NLT). Sadness will not rule the day. Depression will not last forever. The clouds may hide the sun, but they cannot get rid of it. Morning comes. Not as quickly as we want. But morning comes, and with it comes joy.

Do you need this promise? Have you cried a river of tears? Have you lost hope? Do you wonder if morning will ever bring this night to an end? Jesus' friend Mary Magdalene did.

SADNESS WILL NOT RULE THE DAY. DEPRESSION WILL NOT LAST FOREVER.

After Jesus was crucified and he was put in the tomb, Mary Magdalene didn't comprehend his promise. She came looking for a dead Jesus, not a living one. Then she saw that the stone to his tomb had been rolled away and his body was gone. Her world had officially hit rock bottom. Her friend was murdered, and now he was missing.

Have you ever had a moment like this? A moment in which bad news became worse? In which sadness wrapped around you like a fog? In which you came looking for God yet couldn't find him?

If so, you'll love what happened next. In the midst of Mary's darkest moment, the Son came out.

> At this, she turned around and saw Jesus standing there, but she did not realize that it was Jesus.
>
> He asked her, "Woman, why are you crying? Who is it you are looking for?"
>
> Thinking he was the gardener, she said, "Sir, if you have carried him away, tell me where you have put him, and I will get him." (John 20:14–15)

Mary Magdalene didn't recognize her Lord. So Jesus did something about it. He called her by name. "Jesus said to her, 'Mary'" (v. 16).

Mary Magdalene was looking for Jesus, and he found her. In a heartbeat her world went from a dead Jesus to a living one. "Weeping may last through the night, but joy comes with the morning" (Psalm 30:5 NLT).

There will be times when you're tempted to give up. But don't. Open your Bible. Pray to God. Listen to worship music. Talk to trusted friends or family members. Place yourself in a position to be found by Jesus.

Weeping comes. But so does joy. Darkness comes, but so does the morning. Sadness comes, but so does hope. Sorrow may have the night, but it cannot have your life.

GOD'S PROMISES FOR YOU

Do not grieve, for the joy of the LORD is your strength.

NEHEMIAH 8:10

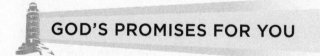

The commandments of the LORD are right,
bringing joy to the heart.
The commands of the LORD are clear,
giving insight for living.

PSALM 19:8 NLT

Wait for the LORD;
be strong and take heart
and wait for the LORD.

PSALM 27:14

Taste and see that the LORD is good.
Oh, the joys of those who take refuge in him!

PSALM 34:8 NLT

Now, Lord, what do I look for?
My hope is in you.

PSALM 39:7

As for me, I watch in hope for the LORD,
I wait for God my Savior;
my God will hear me.

MICAH 7:7

Always be full of joy in the Lord. I say it again—rejoice!

PHILIPPIANS 4:4 NLT

THINK AND RESPOND

Have you ever been through a time when you were overwhelmed with sadness? What were the circumstances?

In the middle of Mary Magdalene's darkest moment, the Son came out. Describe a time when Jesus came into a dark moment and brought light to your situation.

In what areas of your life could you use some joy? Write a prayer asking God to renew your hope.

When you're tempted to give up or it feels like God is distant, there are lots of ways to restore your hope: Read your Bible. Pray to God. Play worship music. Talk with trusted friends or family members. Which of these helps you the most? Why?

MY PROMISE TO GOD

I will seek God even when I am sad. I will remember that God's love for me is endless and unconditional. Any sad times will not last forever, and I will trust him to restore the joy in my heart.

THE HOLY SPIRIT EMPOWERS YOU

"You will receive power when the
Holy Spirit comes on you."

—ACTS 1:8

I have a great bargain for you. It's a tricycle—perfect for your younger brother or sister or the kid next door. Just think of the joy they'll have riding down the sidewalk on this trike. Fire engine red. Tassels that dangle from the handles. And a little bell on the handlebar. I'll sell it to you at one-third of the original price. Of course, there is the small matter of the missing wheel. But the trike still has the other two! And kids need to learn to ride a two-wheeler anyway, right?

Don't be so quick to shake your head. Think about it. One-third off the price for a trike with a missing wheel. Do you not see the value? Of course you don't, and I don't blame you. Who wants two-thirds when you can have the whole?

Yet many Christians settle for a two-thirds God. They rely on the Father and the Son but forget about the Holy Spirit. You wouldn't make that mistake with a trike. You certainly don't want to make that mistake with the Trinity. Ask a believer to answer this question, "Who is God the Father?" He has a reply. Or "Describe God the Son." She immediately knows. But if you want to see Christians search for words, ask, "Who is the Holy Spirit?"

MANY CHRISTIANS SETTLE FOR A TWO-THIRDS GOD. THEY RELY ON THE FATHER AND THE SON BUT FORGET ABOUT THE HOLY SPIRIT.

The Bible makes more than a hundred references to the Holy Spirit. On the eve of Jesus' death, as he prepared his followers to face the future without him, he made this great promise: "You will receive power when the Holy Spirit comes on you" (Acts 1:8).

After Jesus ascended into heaven, the Holy Spirit became the primary agent of the Trinity on earth. He will complete what was begun by the Father and the Son.

The Holy Spirit enters the believer upon confession of faith (Ephesians 1:13). From that point forward the Christian has access to the very power and personality of God. As the Spirit has his way in the lives of believers, a transformation occurs. We begin to think the way God thinks, love the way God loves, and see the way God sees.

This power includes the gifts of the Spirit. "But the Holy Spirit produces this kind of fruit in our lives: love, joy, peace, patience, kindness, goodness, faithfulness, gentleness, and self-control. There is no law against these things!" (Galatians 5:22–23 NLT).

The Spirit of God also makes us *holy.* After all, is he not the *Holy* Spirit? One of his primary activities is to cleanse us from sin and to sanctify us for holy work. Paul reminded the Corinthians: "You were washed, you were sanctified, you were justified in the name of the Lord Jesus Christ and by the Spirit of our God" (1 Corinthians 6:11).

The Holy Spirit is central to the lives of Christians. Everything that happens from the Book of Acts to the end of the Book of Revelation is a result of the work of the Holy Spirit of Christ. The Spirit came alongside the disciples and gave the early church the push that they needed to face the challenges ahead. The Holy Spirit will do the same for you.

Make it your aim to sense, see, and hear the Spirit of God. Take advantage of all God has to offer. Fix your heart on this promise: "You will receive power when the Holy Spirit comes on you" (Acts 1:8).

GOD'S PROMISES FOR YOU

Where can I go from your Spirit?
Where can I flee from your presence?

PSALM 139:7

"When the Spirit of truth comes, he will lead you into all truth. He will not speak his own words, but he will speak only what he hears, and he will tell you what is to come."

JOHN 16:13 NCV

All these are the work of one and the same Spirit, and he distributes them to each one, just as he determines. Just as a body, though one, has many parts, but all its many parts form one body, so it is with Christ. For we were all baptized by one Spirit so as to form one body—whether Jews or Gentiles, slave or free—and we were all given the one Spirit to drink. Even so the body is not made up of one part but of many.

1 CORINTHIANS 12:11–14

The Spirit produces the fruit of love, joy, peace, patience, kindness, goodness, faithfulness, gentleness, self-control.

GALATIANS 5:22–23 NCV

In Christ, God put his special mark of ownership on you by giving you the Holy Spirit that he had promised.

EPHESIANS 1:13 NCV

THINK AND RESPOND

Do you know more about God and Jesus than the Holy Spirit? If so, what are ways you can learn more about this third member of the Trinity?

The Holy Spirit gives you power, creates unity among Christians, guides you in truth, and makes you holy. Now that you know these things, in what ways have you seen the Holy Spirit at work in your life?

Read the gifts of the Spirit listed in Galatians 5:22–23. Which of these gifts have you been given? If you're not sure, pray and ask the Holy Spirit to guide you.

Don't settle for a two-thirds God. List ways the Holy Spirit can help you during the day. After doing that, ask God to give you more awareness of the Holy Spirit's presence during these times.

MY PROMISE TO GOD

I will seek to learn more about and rely on the Holy Spirit. I want to experience more of his gifts and power, so I will spend time getting to know this third member of the Trinity.

JESUS IS BUILDING HIS CHURCH

"On this rock I will build my church, and the power of death will not be able to defeat it."

—MATTHEW 16:18 NCV

Builders build.

Okay, that's pretty basic. But stay with me. I'm, ahem, building up to a point.

I'm writing this at my home. A rock mason named José is at work in our backyard. His face is leathered and his hands are rough. He is building an outdoor fireplace. "I've built a hundred of these," he assured me. Watching José work, I believe it. He has emptied a wheelbarrow of limestone on the courtyard floor. He lifts each rock, studies its shape, and then looks at the fireplace. He then chisels away the unneeded parts until the stone fits the spot. Once the rough edges are gone, he slaps on mortar and sets the rock in place. He is building a fireplace.

In much the same way, Jesus is building his church. Not actual brick-and-mortar walls, but his community of believers. Selecting stones—imperfect people like us. Chiseling away corners to make us more like him. Making this group of people firm with the mortar of faith and his Spirit. He is lifting you from your pile and me from mine and cementing us together. He is building his church.

JESUS IS BUILDING A COMMUNITY OF PEOPLE WHO LOVE HIM WITH ALL THEIR HEARTS.

"*I* will build . . ." Jesus explained. He didn't give this task to someone else. You do not build the church, nor do I. Jesus alone is the Master craftsman.

Yet God's plan has always been this: to use common people for his uncommon cause. We are the hands and feet of Jesus. We are his ambassadors. We are his help for the hungry and his response to the discouraged. Jesus is building a community of people who love him with all their hearts.

His church could have been built without our help. He could have tasked his angels with serving people. Or created a superhuman species of robots to share the good news. He could have picked lions and cheetahs and eagles, but he chose to use people like you and me.

Because God chose people, the church, like people, is imperfect. Satan will try to defeat us. He will divide us for a time, but he will not prevail. If the last two thousand years tell us anything, it's that the church will succeed. How many nations have come and gone? But the church remains. How many armies have risen and fallen? But the church remains. How many systems have been created only to disappear? Yet the church remains.

Jesus will build his church.

When you said yes to Christ, you said yes to his church. We will disagree about lots of things, but there is one thing that unites us: we believe that Jesus Christ is the Son of God. And upon that rock Jesus is building a movement.

All other buildings, from skyscrapers to Legos, will fall. Even my fireplace will crumble someday. But the church of Jesus Christ, built on the person of Jesus, will stand. And you get to help build it.

GOD'S PROMISES FOR YOU

It is good and pleasant
when God's people live together in peace!

PSALM 133:1 NCV

"I am in them and you are in me. May they experience such perfect unity that the world will know that you sent me and that you love them as much as you love me."

JOHN 17:23 NLT

The churches were strengthened in the faith and grew daily in numbers.

ACTS 16:5

I appeal to you, brothers and sisters, in the name of our Lord Jesus Christ, that all of you agree with one another in what you say and that there be no divisions among you, but that you be perfectly united in mind and thought.

1 CORINTHIANS 1:10

Brothers and sisters, what should you do? When you meet together, one person has a song, and another has a teaching. Another has a new truth from God. Another speaks in a different language, and another person interprets that language. The purpose of all these things should be to help the church grow strong.

1 CORINTHIANS 14:26 NCV

THINK AND RESPOND

How do you feel about your local church? Do you love going? Wish you could sleep longer instead? Try to avoid it? Why do you feel the way you do?

How does your view of church differ from Jesus'? What might help you see it more like he does?

God chooses to use imperfect people to help build his church. How does this make you feel? Frustrated with other Christians? Relieved because God can use you?

Jesus wants us each to play a role in building his church. How are you currently doing that? If you aren't, what are ways you could start?

MY PROMISE TO GOD

I will join Jesus in helping build his church. Rather than just showing up, I will use my gifts and talents to serve the church. And I will worship and pray with others in this community knowing that is God's plan for his people.

GOD MEETS ALL YOUR NEEDS

My God will use his wonderful riches in Christ Jesus to give you everything you need.

—PHILIPPIANS 4:19 NCV

There's a popular game called Would You Rather? It challenges you to choose between two outrageous, often gross alternatives. Like, would you rather drink the sweat wrung from your football team's jerseys or trim your grandmother's toenails?

Ready for an easier question? Would you rather be the emperor of Rome or a prisoner of Rome?

It seems obvious that most people would choose the palace over the prison. But rather than wonder which is the better choice, let's look at the lives of two real men in early Rome who lived these alternatives.

We'll start with Nero. He became Emperor of Rome in AD 54 at the age of sixteen. His palace overflowed with servants ready to meet his every need. He wasn't just spoiled; he would kill to get his way. When his mother, Agrippina, wouldn't do as he wished, he had her boat rigged so she would die at sea. Yet she survived. Nero's next plan was simpler. Assassins attacked Agrippina in her home and ended her life.

When Nero was in his twenties, he had a gigantic 120-foot statue built to honor him as a god, yet everyone close to him had been murdered. When he eventually lost power, he took his own life. Rich and powerful, but he died alone. He had everything except happiness.

Now the prisoner. His name was Paul. And unlike Nero, he had nothing but happiness. He was twice the age of Nero, and his tired body carried the marks of whippings, shipwrecks, and disease. His money was gone; his health was failing. In the middle of it all, he ended up in jail, a prisoner of Rome as Nero sat high above in the emperor's mansion. Yet Paul endured suffering because he had the one thing that mattered: he had the Lord.

So back to our question. If you had been a Roman citizen in those days and someone gave you the choice, would you rather be the emperor or the prisoner?

Paul didn't have a palace, but he had faith in God (Philippians 1:13). He wasn't healthy, but he had eternal life (Philippians 1:23). He didn't sleep in a palace, but he slept with a clean conscience (Philippians 3:9). And though he was poor, his heavenly Father was not: "My God will meet all your needs according to the riches of his glory in Christ Jesus" (Philippians 4:19).

THE LORD WILL PROVIDE FOR YOU. HE WILL GIVE YOU EVERYTHING YOU NEED.

Yes! That's the promise. That was the discovery of Paul. That is the Christian hope. God is in charge of your life. The Lord will provide for you. He will give you everything you need.

If you had the choice, if you were offered a palace with no Christ or a prison with Christ, which would you choose? Or, better asked, which are you choosing?

If you have everything but Jesus, you have no life. But if you have nothing but Jesus, you have all the life you need.

GOD'S PROMISES FOR YOU

The poor will eat and be satisfied.
All who seek the LORD will praise him.
Their hearts will rejoice with everlasting joy.

PSALM 22:26 NLT

Even strong young lions sometimes go hungry,
but those who trust in the LORD will lack no good thing.

PSALM 34:10 NLT

God chose things the world considers foolish in order to shame those who think they are wise. And he chose things that are powerless to shame those who are powerful. God chose things despised by the world, things counted as nothing at all, and used them to bring to nothing what the world considers important.

1 CORINTHIANS 1:27–28 NLT

God is able to bless you abundantly, so that in all things at all times, having all that you need, you will abound in every good work.

2 CORINTHIANS 9:8

I want you brothers and sisters to know that what has happened to me has helped to spread the Good News. All the palace guards and everyone else knows that I am in prison because I am a believer in Christ.

PHILIPPIANS 1:12–13 NCV

I do not know what to choose—living or dying. It is hard to choose between the two. I want to leave this life and be with Christ, which is much better, but you need me here in my body.

PHILIPPIANS 1:22–24 NCV

I am right with God, not because I followed the law, but because I believed in Christ. God uses my faith to make me right with him.

PHILIPPIANS 3:9 NCV

THINK AND RESPOND

Do you ever feel like you would be happier if only you had more money, better clothes, or the latest gadget? Why or why not?

Do your choices for Christ sometimes come at a cost? If so, describe a situation when that happened.

Though he was in prison with no money and poor health, Paul had joy. Are you able to hold on to joy in hard times? How?

Read this statement again: "If you have everything but Jesus, you have no life. But if you have nothing but Jesus, you have all the life you need." Have you found this to be true? If so, share why. If not, why not?

MY PROMISE TO GOD

I will trust God to meet my needs in good times and in hard times. I will look to Jesus for my joy rather than comfort or popularity or things money can buy. I know that he alone is what gives my life meaning.

GOD WILL JUDGE THE WORLD

[God] has set a day when he will judge the world.

—ACTS 17:31

Life isn't fair. When did you learn those words? What event showed you how cruel life can be? Did a car wreck leave you fatherless? Did friends forget you, a teacher ignore you, an adult abuse you?

How long will injustices continue? God's answer is direct: Not long. Scripture reveals a serious promise: "[God] has set a day when he will judge the world" (Acts 17:31).

God has not forgotten about or lost interest in making things right. Every flip of the calendar brings us closer to the day in which God will judge all evil.

"Judgment Day" is an unpopular term. We don't like judgment, but we value justice, yet the second is impossible without the first. One can't have justice without judgment. For that reason "we must all appear before the judgment seat of Christ, so that each of us may receive what is due us for the things done while in the body, whether good or bad" (2 Corinthians 5:10).

From his throne Jesus will forever balance the scales of fairness:

1. He will publicly pardon his people. Paul assured the Corinthians "we must all appear before the judgment seat of Christ" (2 Corinthians 5:10). For the sake of justice, Jesus has to expose all of our sinful actions and thoughts. God filters his verdict through Jesus. But we won't stand before the bench alone. Jesus will be at our side.

You won't be embarrassed. To the contrary, you will be stunned. Your awe will grow as the list of forgiven sins lengthens. For every sin, Jesus will say, "I took the punishment for that." And God will make his declaration: not guilty!

2. He will applaud the service of his servants. "He will bring to light what is hidden in darkness and will expose the motives of the heart. At that time each will receive their praise from God" (1 Corinthians 4:5). God will walk you through your life day by day, moment by moment, issuing commendation after commendation. "You gave up your seat on the bus. Well done. You greeted the new student in your class. Fine job. You forgave your brother, encouraged your neighbor . . . I'm so proud of you."

God records and rewards your goodness. It's only fair that he does. And since he is a just God, he will pardon his people, applaud the service of his servants, and . . .

3. He will honor the wishes of the wicked. Some people will stand before God who "didn't treat him like God, refusing to worship him . . . they traded the glory of God who holds the whole world in his hands for cheap figurines you can buy at any roadside stand" (Romans 1:21, 23 THE MESSAGE). They spent a lifetime dishonoring the King and hurting his people. A just God must honor the wishes of God-rejecters.

GOD UNDERSTANDS INJUSTICE. HE WILL RIGHT ALL WRONGS AND HEAL ALL WOUNDS.

When you wonder if the wicked will go unpunished or injustices will go unaddressed, let this promise satisfy your desire for justice. God will have the final word.

God understands injustice. He will right all wrongs and heal all wounds. He has prepared a place where life will be finally and forever . . . just.

GOD'S PROMISES FOR YOU

You reward everyone
according to what they have done.

PSALM 62:12

"The Son of Man is going to come in his Father's glory with his angels, and then he will reward each person according to what they have done."

MATTHEW 16:27

"The master answered, 'You did well. You are a good and loyal servant. Because you were loyal with small things, I will let you care for much greater things. Come and share my joy with me.'"

MATTHEW 25:23 NCV

Do not judge before the right time; wait until the Lord comes. He will bring to light things that are now hidden in darkness, and will make known the secret purposes of people's hearts. Then God will praise each one of them.

1 CORINTHIANS 4:5 NCV

We must all stand before Christ to be judged. We will each receive whatever we deserve for the good or evil we have done in this earthly body.

2 CORINTHIANS 5:10 NLT

I saw a great white throne and him who was seated on it. The earth and the heavens fled from his presence, and there was no place for them. And I saw the dead, great and small, standing before the throne, and books were opened. Another book was opened, which is the book of life. The dead were judged according to what they had done as recorded in the books.

REVELATION 20:11-12

"Look, I am coming soon! My reward is with me, and I will give to each person according to what they have done."

REVELATION 22:12

THINK AND RESPOND

Identify something in your life that wasn't fair. How did this event make you feel? Did it affect the way you view God?

Does God's Day of Judgment bring you a sense of comfort, fear, or a mix of both? Explain why.

Do you know that all of your sins have been completely forgiven and paid for by Jesus? How does that affect your view of judgment?

On Judgment Day you will not only be judged for your wrongs, but your good deeds will be recognized. Knowing that God sees everything you do, how are you encouraged to do good even if you're never recognized for it on earth?

MY PROMISE TO GOD

In a world with so many injustices, I know a time is coming when God will make everything right. I will respect God's justice and delight in his grace now and on the Day of Judgment, knowing my sins are completely forgiven and paid for by Jesus.

GOD MAKES ALL THINGS NEW

"I am making everything new!"

—REVELATION 21:5

When did you first notice how busy and overcrowded this world is? The school has no space for you. Your mother's schedule has no space for you. Your friends don't have space for you. So you get ignored, cut, or pushed aside.

You were made for a more spacious life. We just don't experience it much here. See if John's words about your true home—literally heaven on earth—don't cause your heart to beat a bit faster.

"I, John, saw the Holy City, the new Jerusalem, coming down from God out of heaven. It was a glorious sight, beautiful as a bride at her wedding" (Revelation 21:2 TLB).

Having just provided this image of the new heaven and new earth, he tries to describe the new city. Look how excited he is: "I, John, saw the holy city . . . ." John spoke with the breathless enthusiasm of a child telling his parents what he saw at the zoo.

Why should a New Jerusalem interest us? John offers two good reasons.

God has space for us.

> The angel who talked to me held in his hand a gold measuring stick to measure the city, its gates, and its wall. When he measured it, he found it was a square, as wide as it was long. In fact, its length and width and height were each 1,400 miles. Then he measured the walls and found them to be 216 feet thick (according to the human standard used by the angel). (Revelation 21:15–17 NLT)

Forget any worries of spending eternity in a cramped space. The size of the New Jerusalem stretches the imagination: 1,400 miles in length, width, and height. Forty times the size of England. Ten times the size of France and larger than India. And that's just the ground floor! The city stands as tall as it does wide. Supposing God stacks the city in stories as an architect would a building, the New Jerusalem would have 600,000 floors, enough space for billions of people. We won't be squished, that's for sure.

But God doesn't just have space for us. God has grace for us.

> She had a great and high wall with twelve gates . . . and names written on them, which are the names of the twelve tribes of the children of Israel . . . the wall of the city had twelve foundations, and on them were the names of the twelve apostles of the Lamb. (Revelation 21:12, 14 NKJV)

These names of imperfect people show God remembers those who love and serve him.

But he has something even better than that. He gives this promise for what is to come. "I am making everything new!" (Revelation 21:5). Imagine everyone and everything you love—being like new again for all eternity. No more struggles. No more shame before God. No more tension between people. No more death.

EVERY PAGE AND PROMISE OF THE BIBLE INVITES AND EXCITES US WITH THE LURE OF A NEW DAY, A NEW EARTH, AND A NEW KINGDOM.

Every page and promise of the Bible invites and excites us with the lure of a new day, a new earth, and a new kingdom. One with plenty of space for you!

GOD'S PROMISES FOR YOU

The created world itself can hardly wait for what's coming next.

ROMANS 8:19 THE MESSAGE

We do not give up. Our physical body is becoming older and weaker, but our spirit inside us is made new every day. We have small troubles for a while now, but they are helping us gain an eternal glory that is much greater than the troubles. We set our eyes not on what we see but on what we cannot see. What we see will last only a short time, but what we cannot see will last forever.

2 CORINTHIANS 4:16–18 NCV

Think about the things of heaven, not the things of earth.

COLOSSIANS 3:2 NLT

"I am making everything new!"

REVELATION 21:5

The angel showed me the river of the water of life. It was shining like crystal and was flowing from the throne of God and of the Lamb down the middle of the street of the city. The tree of life was on each side of the river. It produces fruit twelve times a year, once each month. The leaves of the tree are for the healing of all the nations. Nothing that God judges guilty will be in that city. The throne of God and of the Lamb will be there, and God's servants will worship him.

REVELATION 22:1–3 NCV

THINK AND RESPOND

On this earth there's only so much time, only room for so many students, only so many seats. In what areas of your life (school, home, social media, friends, curfew, and so on) could you use more space? Why?

Heaven will have both space and grace for you. How does that make you feel? Why are both important?

John describes the New Jerusalem, when it comes down out of heaven, as a bride dressed for her husband. What do you think John means by that image?

The promise of making everything new (Revelation 21:5) is breathtaking. Who or what are you most looking forward to seeing made new? Why?

MY PROMISE TO GOD

I will fix my eyes on things above. I will hold to the promise of all things being made new when God makes everything right. I look forward to experiencing the beauty, space, and grace of heaven.

HOPE IS THE ANCHOR OF YOUR SOUL

We have this hope as an anchor for the soul, firm and secure.

—HEBREWS 6:19

It doesn't matter whether you see a half-empty glass as half full. Sometimes we all run short on hope.

When you feel hope fading, where do you turn?

I think the best place to turn is to this great promise: "We have this hope as an anchor for the soul, firm and secure. It enters the inner sanctuary behind the curtain, where our forerunner, Jesus, has entered on our behalf" (Hebrews 6:19–20).

Look at the key terms of the first phrase: *anchor* and *soul.*

You don't need to be told what an anchor is. You've held those iron castings with the pointed edges. Perhaps you've thrown one from a boat into the water and felt the yank as the tool found its lodging place. The anchor has one purpose—to steady the boat. You need one that can hook securely to an object that is stronger than the storm. You need a good anchor.

Why? Because you have a valuable vessel. You have a soul. When God breathed into Adam, he gave him more than oxygen; he gave him an eternal being. He gave him a soul.

BUILD YOUR LIFE ON THE PROMISES OF GOD. SINCE HIS PROMISES ARE UNBREAKABLE, YOUR HOPE WILL BE UNSHAKABLE.

The presence of a soul separates you from your pet goldfish. Both of you eat. Both of you have eyes and scales—his on his skin, yours on the bathroom floor. Though the two of you are much alike, there is one huge difference—the soul.

Because of your soul, you wonder why you are here. Because of your soul, you wonder where you are going. Because of your soul, you wrestle with right and wrong. You value the lives of others. Goldfish don't do these things.

Your soul separates you from animals and unites you to God. And your soul needs an anchor. This anchor is set, not on another boat, or person, or possession. No, this anchor is set in the "inner sanctuary behind the curtain, where our forerunner, Jesus, has entered on our behalf" (Hebrews 6:20).

Our anchor, in other words, is set in the very throne room of God. We might imagine the anchor attached to the throne itself. It will never break free. The rope will never snap. The anchor is set, and the rope is strong. Why? Because it is beyond the reach of the devil and under the care of Christ. Since no one can take your Christ, no one can take your hope.

Ask yourself this key question: *Is what I'm hooked to stronger than what I'll go through?* When the storm hits, trust no one but God. The apostle Paul proclaimed it triumphantly: "We have put our hope in the living God" (1 Timothy 4:10).

In the first chapter, I told you that the promises here in this book are some of my favorites. They are a handful of the ones I've treasured throughout the years. Now that I've shared my list, I urge you to create your own.

The best book of promises is the one that you and God are going write together. Search and search until you find the ones that match your needs. When the enemy comes with his lies of doubt and fear, repeat them out loud. Satan will be quickly silenced. He has no reply for truth.

Build your life on the promises of God. Since his promises are unbreakable, your hope will be unshakable. The winds will still blow. The rain will still fall. But, in the end, your anchor will hold, your soul will be well, and you'll be standing on solid ground with the promises of God.

GOD'S PROMISES FOR YOU

Always pray and never lose hope.

LUKE 18:1 NCV

There is no condemnation for those who belong to Christ Jesus.

ROMANS 8:1 NLT

In this hope we were saved. But hope that is seen is no hope at all. Who hopes for what they already have?

ROMANS 8:24

Who then will condemn us? No one—for Christ Jesus died for us and was raised to life for us, and he is sitting in the place of honor at God's right hand, pleading for us.

ROMANS 8:34 NLT

May the God of hope fill you with all joy and peace as you trust in him, so that you may overflow with hope by the power of the Holy Spirit.

ROMANS 15:13

This is why we work hard and continue to struggle, for our hope is in the living God, who is the Savior of all people and particularly of all believers.

1 TIMOTHY 4:10 NLT

Our high priest is able to understand our weaknesses.

HEBREWS 4:15 NCV

THINK AND RESPOND

When do you tend to lose hope most? Why do you think it happens during those times?

In the past when troubles came, did you anchor your hope to other people or things? Name those faulty anchors. How did it work out? How would the circumstances have been different if you had anchored your hope in God?

How do God's promises act as the only trustworthy anchors for your soul (Hebrews 6:19–20)?

Do you have a journal or book where you can write your struggles, victories, and the promises from God that act as the anchor for your soul? If not, will you plan to get one? What will your first journal entry be?

MY PROMISE TO GOD

I will anchor my soul to the hope of Christ. When shaky situations come, I will remember the unbreakable promises of God and not be shaken.

NOTES

1. "Religion: Promises," *Time*, December 24, 1956, http://content.time.com/time/magazine/article/0,9171,808851,00.html.
2. Louis J. Cameli, *The Devil You Don't Know: Recognizing and Resisting Evil in Everyday Life* (Notre Dame, IN: Ave Maria Press, 2011), 79.
3. "Most American Christians Do Not Believe That Satan or the Holy Spirit Exist," Barna, April 13, 2009, https://www.barna.com/research/most-american-christians-do-not-believe-that-satan-or-the-holy-spirit-exist/.
4. Jeane MacIntosh, "Homeless Heir to Huguette Clark's $19M Fortune Found Dead in Wyoming," *New York Post*, December 31, 2012, https://nypost.com/2012/12/31/homeless-heir-to-huguette-clarks-19m-fortune-found-dead-in-wyoming/.